READING IN THE CONTENT AREAS
SOCIAL STUDIES 1

Laura Stark Johnson

PERMISSIONS

A. J. S. PUBLICATIONS, INC. for "The Lawmaking Process" from *Our Federal and State Constitutions* by Alex J. Schmidt. Published by A. J. S. Publications, Inc., Island Lake, IL 60042, (312) 526-5027, 1989.

DANIEL J. BOORSTIN for "A Democracy of Clothing" from *The Landmark History of the American People,* by Daniel J. Boorstin, Vol. 2, pp. 25–30 (newly revised and updated, 1987). Copyright 1970, 1987 by Daniel J. Boorstin. Published by Random House, New York. Reprinted by permission.

ENCYCLOPAEDIA BRITANNICA, INC. for "Mountains." Reprinted with permission from *Britannica Junior Encyclopaedia,* © 1972 by Encyclopaedia Britannica, Inc.

FRANKLIN WATTS for "The Bill of Rights: Safeguard of Freedom" from *The Bill of Rights* by E. B. Fincher. Published by Franklin Watts, New York. Copyright 1987 by Watts.

G. P. PUTNAM'S SONS for excerpt from "Shh! We're Writing the Constitution." From *Shh! We're Writing the Constitution* by Jean Fritz, text copyright © 1987 by Jean Fritz. Reprinted by permission of G. P. Putnam's Sons.

GROLIER INC. for "The Industrial Revolution." Reprinted with permission of *The New Book of Knowledge,* 1990 edition, © Grolier Inc.

PLATT & MUNK, PUBLISHERS for "The Objective" from *To the Top of the World* by Mark Sufrin, copyright © 1966 by Platt & Munk, Publishers. Reprinted by permission of Platt & Munk, Publishers.

WADSWORTH, INC. for "How People Use Space and Time." From *Communicate! 3/E* by Rudolph F. Verderber, © 1981 by Wadsworth, Inc. © 1975, 1978 by Wadsworth Publishing Company, Inc. Reprinted by permission of the publisher.

GRACE W. WEINSTEIN for "Making Ends Meet." From *Public Affairs Pamphlet No. 624: Making Ends Meet,* March 1984, by Grace W. Weinstein.

WESTERN PUBLISHING COMPANY, INC. for "A Century of Freedom." From *The Golden Book of the History of the United States* by Earl Schenck Miers © 1970, 1963 Western Publishing Company, Inc. & Ridge Press, Inc. Used by Permission.

for "Maps." From *The Golden Book Encyclopedia* © 1988 Western Publishing Company, Inc. Used by permission.

WILLIAM MORROW AND COMPANY, INC. for "The Little Factory Girl to a More Fortunate Playmate," from *Saturday's Children: Poems of Work,* ed. Helen Plotz. New York: Greenwillow Books, 1982.

Every effort has been made to locate the persons or agencies authorized to give permission to reprint the selection "Poor Richard" from *The Rainbow Book of American History* by Earl Schenck Miers.

ISBN 0-88336-115-9

©1991

New Readers Press
Publishing Division of Laubach Literacy International
Box 131, Syracuse, New York 13210

Printed in the United States of America

Project Editor: Christina M. Jagger
Manuscript Editor: Margaret Duckett
Publication Assistant: Heidi Stephens
Cover Design: Patricia Rapple
Cover Art: Stephen Rhodes

9 8 7 6 5 4 3 2

Table of Contents

Unit 1: Geography

the study of the earth's surface, climates, peoples, and natural resources

ROCKY MOUNTAINS IN THE SELKIRK RANGE NEAR THE CANADIAN BORDER
(MOUNT SIR DONALD), c. 1889, Albert Bierstadt, collection of Free Public Library,
New Bedford, Massachusetts.

Why do people use maps? One reason is to get where they want to go. Maps were not always as accurate as they are today. Columbus came to the Americas as a result of an error in a map. Read the following selection to discover more about maps.

Maps

What is the easiest way to drive from Chicago to Denver? How many countries are on the continent of Asia? What is Japan's main food crop? These questions can be answered by using maps. A map is a drawing or diagram of all of the earth or a part of it.

Kinds of Maps

There are hundreds of kinds of maps. A *road map* helps drivers get where they want to go. The map shows how far different places are from each other. It shows which roads go directly from one place to another. A road map gives the names of streets, towns, and cities.

Ship captains and airplane pilots use maps called *charts*. A sailor's chart shows the shoreline and the depth of the water. It helps the captain pick a safe, short route. An air chart shows where cities and airports are. It also shows where planes of different kinds are allowed to fly.

A book of maps is called an *atlas*. The maps in an atlas may show the locations of the countries of the world. The maps also show oceans and seas, rivers and lakes, mountains, towns, and many other features.

Some maps in an atlas describe the land. They may show where there are forests or swamps. They may show a region's natural resources, such as oil and minerals. Other atlas maps show where people live. Still others may show what people do with the land—where certain crops are grown or where certain products are produced.

A special kind of world map called a *globe* shows Earth as it is—a sphere. A globe is actually made by drawing the map on triangular strips of paper and then pasting them to a round ball. Yet because of its shape, a globe shows the sizes and positions of landmasses and bodies of water more accurately than a flat map.

History

People have been making maps for more than 16,000 years. The Babylonians made maps on stone tablets before 1000 B.C. Later, the Phoenicians, Egyptians, and Persians made maps, too. These early maps were not very accurate, because early peoples did not travel very much. They knew only about nearby regions.

The maps of the ancient Greeks were more scientific. The Greeks gathered information from travelers from distant places. They noticed that in different places, the sun, moon, and stars appeared in different parts of the sky. They used this information to tell directions and measure distances.

One of the early Greek mapmakers was Eratosthenes, who lived in the 200s B.C. He thought the world was round, and that it measured about 28,000 miles around the equator. He was close. The actual distance around

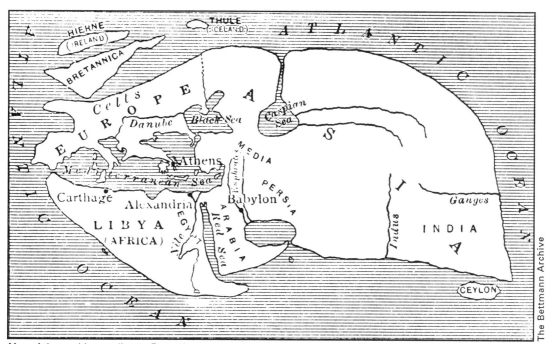

Map of the world according to Eratosthenes.

The Bettmann Archive

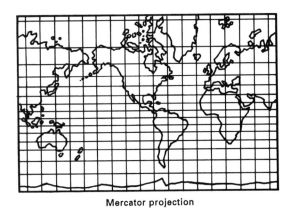
Mercator projection

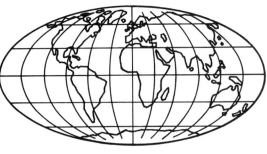
Mollweide projection

Projections help show a part of the round earth as accurately as possible on a flat map. The Mercator projection (left) is good for small areas. But if you show the whole world, Antarctica looks like a long strip of land instead of a continent! The Mollweide projection (right) is better for large areas.

the equator is 24,901 miles (40,075 kilometers[1]). He was also one of the first mapmakers to use lines of latitude[2] and longitude.[3]

Another Greek mapmaker, Ptolemy, believed that the earth was round, too. But he saw this as a problem for a mapmaker. How can you draw a map of a round surface on a flat surface? To understand this problem, cut an orange down one side and scoop the fruit out, leaving the peel whole. Open the peel out, then try to lay it flat.

Ptolemy figured out ways to draw maps of a curved surface on a flat surface. These special ways of drawing are called *projections*.[4] Maps today use many kinds of projections.

Ptolemy's maps were the best in the world for more than 1,000 years. But they had errors. In the 1400s, Ptolemy's maps led Christopher Columbus to believe Asia was only a few thousand miles west of Spain. But Asia was actually thousands of miles farther west. Columbus discovered the Americas as a result of this mistake.

Columbus and other explorers learned many new facts that improved maps. Some mapmakers even went on voyages themselves. They watched the sun, moon, and stars to keep track of where they were. They sailed along coastlines and drew their shapes. The first globes were made in the late 1400s.

How Maps Are Made

Mapmakers draw what they see or what other people tell them. Suppose you wanted to draw a map of the streets and buildings in your neighborhood. First, you would go out and see where the streets run and how they cross. You would take measurements and note the location of buildings. There might be a service station on

1. **kilometer:** a unit of length in the metric system that is equal to 1,000 meters or about 5/8 of a mile.
2. **latitude:** imaginary lines used to measure distance north or south of the equator.
3. **longitude:** imaginary lines used to measure distance east or west of the prime meridian. The prime meridian is an imaginary line that runs from the North Pole to the South Pole.
4. **projections:** the transferring of east-west lines and north-south lines from a globe onto a flat map.

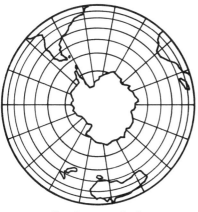

Equal–area projection

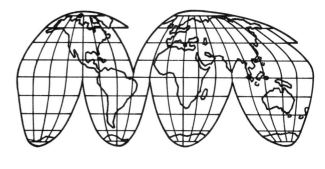

Goode's interrupted homolosine

The equal-area projection (left) looks down on Antarctica. It gives a true picture of the area, but not necessarily a true shape. The Goode projection at right is very good at showing shapes and areas near the equator. But it breaks the oceans into pieces and makes Antarctica look like four separate pieces of land.

one street corner and a restaurant on another. When you had all this information, you could draw your map.

Professional mapmakers have special tools. One important tool is a compass. A compass always points in the same direction—north. On most maps, north is at the top of the map, and south is at the bottom.

Mapmakers also use surveying instruments. These help measure distances on land and the height of hills or mountains. Surveyors and mapmakers use *geometry*—a kind of mathematics. The word *geometry* comes from Greek words meaning "earth measurement."

Mapmakers take special cameras up in airplanes so that they can photograph a town or region. Fitting the pictures together provides useful information for a map. Satellites high above Earth take pictures of large areas of the planet. These can be used to make maps, too.

Photo maps have many uses. Scientists know oil is often found under certain land formations. Photo maps help them see these land formations. Satellite and airplane photos are also helpful in making weather maps and predicting the weather.

Reading Maps

Mapmakers have several ways of showing information. One of the most important is color or shading. For example, on a *political map*[5] of the United States, colors may be used to show the different states. No states that border each other are the same color. On a map of a single state, color may be used to show *elevations*—how high the land is above sea level. On a map about living things, colors may show where different plants grow.

Mapmakers also use symbols. The symbols are usually explained in a box near the map's border. It includes a *scale* and a *legend*. When you understand the legend and the scale, you can read the map.

---

5. political map: a map that emphasizes boundaries of counties, states, or countries.

The map's legend tells what its colors, symbols, and lines mean. On some maps, for example, a star represents the capital of a country or state. A large circle stands for a large town, and a small circle for a small town. A red line means a major highway, and an airplane may stand for an airport.

The scale tells you how to figure actual distances from distances used on the map. For example, on a map of a city, the scale may say "1 inch = 1 mile." If the map is 8 inches across, then the map shows a region that is actually 8 miles across. On a map of the whole world, the scale might say "1 inch = 3,000 miles"!

Suppose you want to know the distance between two cities on a map with a scale of "1 inch = 10 miles." First, measure the distance on the map with a ruler. If the cities are 4 inches apart, then they are actually 40 miles apart.

Many flat maps are crossed by grid lines that divide the map into boxes of equal size. Along the left and right edges of the map, the boxes are labeled with letters—A, B, C, and so on. Along the top and bottom edges, the boxes are labeled with numbers—1, 2, 3, and so on. The labeled boxes help you find places named in the map's *index*. The index is a list of places shown on the map, along with directions telling you which box to look in to find each place. For example, after a town name, the map index may say "G-5." To find the town on the map, find the row of boxes labeled G. Then find the column of boxes labeled 5. The box where these two cross is "G-5." The town you are looking for will be in that box.

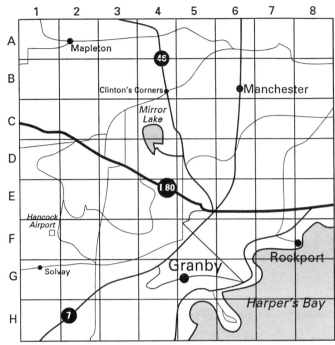

Look at the map above. What town is located in G-5?

From *The Golden Book Encyclopedia*.

Do you enjoy looking at a globe? The spin of a globe reveals that much of the world's surface is water. Read the following selection to discover more interesting facts about the world.

The World

The world is the planet earth viewed especially as the home of human beings and other living things. The earth is just one of countless heavenly bodies in the universe. But it is the only one known to support life.

From the very beginning of their life on the earth, people have had to adapt to conditions in the world to survive. The earliest human beings lived by hunting and gathering wild plants. They made clothing from animal hides and furs and used branches and other natural materials to build shelters. About 10,000 years ago, some people began to raise plants and animals after food became scarce. People who farmed could settle in one place and produce enough food to feed many others. Villages grew up, and people developed methods of living in large groups. New occupations and forms of government became necessary. Over the years, people created more advanced technology and increasingly complicated forms of social life.

They built great cities, developed civilizations, and found ways to control many powerful natural forces.

The world's surface consists of water and land. Air surrounds the surface and extends to outer space. Water—chiefly the great oceans—covers about 70 percent of the world's surface. All living things must have water to live, just as they must have air. People also use water for irrigation, industry, power, and transportation. In addition, the oceans, lakes, and rivers provide fish and other foods.

The oceans separate huge landmasses called *continents*. Most of the world's countries lie on the continents. Others are on islands. Each country has its own political and economic systems. However, countries cooperate with one another in many ways. For example, they make trade agreements and sign treaties designed to reduce the likelihood of war.

The physical features of a country strongly influence where the people of that country live. People can most easily grow food on plains or in river valleys, where the soil is rich and deep. Mountainous regions generally are not suitable for crop farming because the soil is thin and easily washed away by rainfall. Many of the world's biggest cities began as important trading centers on seacoasts, lakeshores, and riverbanks. Thus, the majority of the world's people live on flat, fertile plains and in large cities that border major water transportation routes.

About 5 1/4 billion people live in the world. They are distributed unevenly over the land. Many areas are heavily populated. Other areas have no people at all. The population is increasing far more rapidly in some countries than in others.

All the world's people belong to the same species, *Homo sapiens,* which means they have a common ancestry.

But many groups of people have lived apart for such a long time that they have developed certain physical variations. Members of the same group, or *race,* resemble one another more than they resemble members of other races. In some cases, physical appearance—such as the color of the skin or the shape of the eyes—can identify members of a race. However, many scientists use blood groups and other characteristics of body chemistry in comparing races.

Nations of the World

In 1990, the world had 170 independent countries and 47 dependencies. An independent country controls its own affairs. Dependencies are controlled in some way by independent countries.

Throughout history, the political map of the world has changed repeatedly. The most important changes have resulted from major wars.

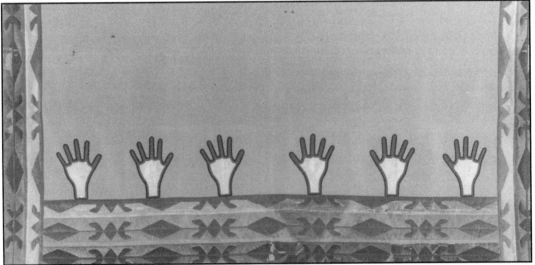

Detail from Osage Friendship Blanket, Native American, 18th century, courtesy of the Cranbrook Institute of Science, Bloomfield Hills, Michigan.

World War I (1914–1918) and World War II (1939–1945) resulted in many important changes on the world map. World War I led to the formation of a number of new nations in Europe. These nations included Austria, Czechoslovakia, Hungary, and Yugoslavia. After World War II, several nations gained or lost territory, and many new nations were established in Asia. In Africa, a strong movement for independence swept the continent. More than 45 African colonies have gained independence since the 1950s.

People of the World

Population. In 1990, the world's population totaled about 5 1/4 billion. The yearly rate of population growth during the late 1980s was about 1.7 percent. At that rate, the world's population would double every 41 years.

If all the world's people were distributed evenly over the land, about 100 people would live on every square mile (39 on every square kilometer). However, the world's people are not distributed evenly, and so the *population density* (the average number of people in a specific area) varies greatly. Some regions, including Antarctica and certain desert areas, have no permanent settlers at all.

The most densely populated regions of the world are in Europe and in southern and eastern Asia. North America has heavy concentrations of people in the northeastern and central regions and along the Pacific coast. Africa, Australia, and South America have densely populated areas near the coasts. The interiors of those continents are thinly settled.

Just as the population density varies from one part of the world to another, so does the rate of population growth. Developing countries generally have higher average rates of increase than developed nations. Africa has a population growth rate of 3.0 percent yearly, the highest of all continents. South America's rate of increase—2.1 percent—is also high. Asia's rate is 1.8 percent, North America's is 0.8 percent, and Australia's is 1.2 percent. Europe has the lowest rate of increase, only 0.2 percent.

Population

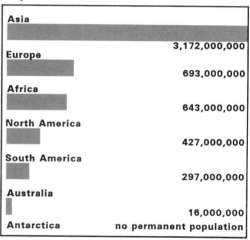

Asia	3,172,000,000
Europe	693,000,000
Africa	643,000,000
North America	427,000,000
South America	297,000,000
Australia	16,000,000
Antarctica	no permanent population

The world's largest country in terms of population is China, which has more than a billion people. India ranks second largest, followed in descending order by the Soviet Union, the United States, Indonesia, and Brazil. More than half the world's people live in these six nations. Vatican City has the smallest population of any of the world's nations. It has only about 1,000 people.

Languages. There are about 3,000 spoken languages in the world. However, only 12 are widely used. Each of these languages is spoken by over 100 million people. More people speak Chinese than any other language. English ranks second, followed by Russian, Spanish, Hindi, Arabic, Bengali, Portuguese, Japanese, German, Malay-Indonesian, and French.

Physical Features of the World

The surface area of the world totals about 196,951,000 square miles (510,100,000 square kilometers). Water covers about 139,692,000 square miles (361,800,000 square kilometers), or about 70 percent of the world's surface. Only about 30 percent consists of land, which covers about 57,259,000 square miles (148,300,000 square kilometers).

The physical geography of a specific region includes the region's surface features and climate. It also includes the soil, mineral deposits, plant and animal life, and other natural resources. Physical geography thus helps determine the economy of a region and how people in the region live.

Water. Oceans, lakes, and rivers make up most of the water that covers the surface of the world. The water surface consists chiefly of three large oceans—the Pacific, the Atlantic, and the Indian. The Pacific Ocean is the largest. It covers about 63,800,000 square miles (165,200,000 square

kilometers), or about a third of the world's surface. The Atlantic Ocean is about half as large as the Pacific, and the Indian Ocean is slightly smaller than the Atlantic. These three oceans come together around Antarctica. The Atlantic and the Pacific meet again near the North Pole, where they form the Arctic Ocean.

The World's Surface

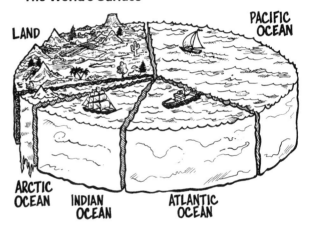

The world's largest lake is the Caspian Sea, a body of salt water that lies between Asia and Europe east of the Caucasus Mountains. The Caspian covers about 143,630 square miles (372,000 square kilometers). The world's largest body of fresh water is the Great Lakes in North America. These five lakes—Erie, Huron, Michigan, Ontario, and Superior—are interconnected, and so they are often referred to as one body of water. Together, they cover about 94,510 square miles (244,780 square kilometers).

The longest river in the world is the Nile in Africa, which flows 4,145 miles (6,671 kilometers). The second longest river, the Amazon in South America, has a length of 4,000 miles (6,437 kilometers). The Mississippi is the longest river in the United States. It flows 2,348 miles (3,779 kilometers).

All living things need water to stay alive. People obtain drinking water from rivers, freshwater lakes, and wells. We also require water for our way of life. We use water in our homes for cleaning and cooking. The manufacture of almost all our products requires water. In dry regions, farmers draw water from rivers, lakes, and wells to irrigate crops. Oceans, lakes, and rivers supply us with fish and other foods.

Water is also a source of power. The force of falling water from rivers, waterfalls, and dams can be used to generate hydroelectricity. In such countries as Brazil and Norway, hydroelectric power stations supply nearly all the electricity used in industry and homes.

The waters of the world also serve as major transportation routes. Every day, thousands of cargo ships cross the oceans, sail along seacoasts, and travel on inland waters. A nation's location along a seacoast can have a powerful influence on its progress and prosperity.[1] The United States, Great Britain, Japan, and some other leading trading nations have long coastlines. Many of the world's major cities border important water transportation routes.

Land. The land area of the world consists of seven continents and many thousands of islands. Asia is the largest

continent, followed by Africa, North America, South America, Antarctica, Europe, and Australia. Geographers sometimes refer to Europe and Asia as one continent called *Eurasia.*

The world's land surface includes mountains, plateaus,[2] hills, valleys, and plains. Relatively few people live in mountainous areas or on high plateaus. Most such regions are too cold, rugged, or dry for comfortable living or for crop farming and other human activities. The soil is poor and easily washed away by rain. However, some mountain valleys and high grassy plateaus serve as grazing land for cattle, sheep, and other livestock. The majority of the world's people live on plains or in hilly regions. Most plains and hilly regions have excellent soil and an abundant water supply. They are good regions for farming, manufacturing, and trade. Many areas unsuitable for farming, particularly mountainous regions, have plentiful mineral resources. Some desert areas, especially in the Middle East, have large deposits of petroleum.

A region's natural resources influence its economic development. The Pampa, a grassy plain in central Argentina, has excellent pastureland for raising cattle and rich soil for growing wheat. Beef and wheat make up Argentina's leading exports. Great Britain lacks enough good farmland to support all its people, but large deposits of coal and iron ore have helped make the country an industrial power. Such countries as the United

---

1. **prosperity:** success.
2. **plateaus:** broad stretches of high, level land.

States, Canada, and the Soviet Union have a variety and abundance of natural resources, which have helped make them become economic giants.

Threats to the environment. For centuries, people have used the world's natural resources to make their lives more comfortable. However, these resources are not always used wisely. Thus, many problems have resulted that threaten the environment.

Many water supplies have become polluted by sewage, industrial chemicals, and other wastes. The burning of fuel in motor vehicles, factories, and furnaces has caused air pollution in numerous cities. Forest regions have been stripped of large areas of trees, resulting in soil erosion[3] and the destruction of animal life. Certain farming practices, including the use of chemical fertilizers and pesticides, have polluted the soil. Many farmers plant the same crop in a field year after year, which reduces the soil's fertility.

Since the mid-1900s, people have become increasingly aware of the need to protect their environment. Local and national governments have passed laws to control the use of natural resources. But it takes many years to renew a water supply, grow a forest, or replace a layer of topsoil. People must practice conservation continuously to repair damage that has already occurred and to prevent future problems.

---

3. **erosion:** wearing away.

Interesting Facts About the World

Area of the world's surface is about 196,951,000 square miles (510,100,000 square kilometers).

Population of the world in 1990 totaled about 5,288,000,000.

Largest continent is Asia, which covers 16,956,000 square miles (43,917,000 square kilometers).

Smallest continent is Australia, which covers 2,966,150 square miles (7,682,300 square kilometers).

Largest country is the Soviet Union, which covers 8,649,500 square miles (22,402,000 square kilometers).

Smallest country is Vatican City. It has an area of only 1/6 square mile (0.4 square kilometer).

Most populous country is China, which had about 1,100,000,000 people in 1990.

Least populous country, Vatican City, had only about 1,000 citizens in 1990.

Highest point in the world, Mount Everest in Asia, rises 29,028 feet (8,848 meters) above sea level.

Lowest point on land is the shore of the Dead Sea in Asia. It lies 1,310 feet (399 meters) below sea level.

Deepest point in the world's oceans is Challenger Deep, 36,198 feet (11,033 meters) below the surface of the Pacific Ocean southwest of Guam in the Mariana Trench.

Excerpted from *The World Book Encyclopedia.*
© 1990 World Book, Inc. By permission of the publisher.

Why are mountains fascinating? Some people enjoy their breathtaking view. Other people enjoy the challenge of climbing mountains. As you read the following selection, think about other reasons why mountains fascinate people.

ANCIENT GEOLOGY, 1987, Karen Kunc, Jan Cicero Gallery, Chicago, Illinois.

Mountains

Because of their great size and grandeur, mountains have always been thought of as having unchanging strength. Men have written of them as "the everlasting hills." The geologist[1] who studies mountains has proof, however, that they are not everlasting. They were formed by certain changes in the earth and are being slowly but surely destroyed by other changes. Boulders are broken from mountain sides by freezing water; soil and rock particles are carried away by rainwash and streams. The deep valleys and canyons in many mountain ranges show the wearing away, or erosion, that takes place all the time. In time even the highest mountains are thus changed to rolling hills or plains.

The rocky Laurentian plains of eastern Canada and the rolling low hills of New England are all that are left of once high mountains in those areas. The great height of the Himalayas shows that those mountains are young. There the rising up of the high slopes happened so recently that they are not yet worn down. Many great ranges, including the Alps and Himalayas, are made largely of rock that was once under the sea. The rocks have in them the fossil remains of sea animals.

---

1. geologist: a person who studies the history and structure of the earth, especially as recorded in rocks.

Although mountains are found on all the continents, many of the greatest ranges belong to one or the other of two great belts. One belt surrounds the Pacific Ocean, and includes western North and South America, Alaska, and eastern Asia, Japan, and Australia. The other belt crosses the East Indies, southern Asia, and the Mediterranean region of Europe, including the Himalayas, Caucasus, Alps, and Pyrenees.

How Mountains Are Formed

Mountains are classified by geologists according to how they were formed. *Folded mountains* were made of rock layers that had been squeezed by very great pressure into large folds. The wearing away, or erosion, of these mountains has often made valleys in and across folded ranges. In many places rock layers may be seen curving up and down in arches and dips. The Appalachian Mountains of the valley-and-ridge region of eastern United States and the Alps of Europe are fine examples of folded mountains.

In *dome mountains* the rock layers have been forced up into great blister-like domes. Many small domes up to a few miles across have been lifted by molten lava. This lava was forced up between the layers of rock from below by vast pressures. As domes are worn away, or eroded, the inner rocks may be quite different from those around the edges. The Black Hills of South Dakota are examples of large domes. The Henry Mountains of Utah are examples of small domes.

Block mountains are the result of breaks, or *faults*, in the earth's crust.

Huge parts of the earth's surface have been raised up or tilted. In the Great Basin in Nevada, hundreds of such blocks of rock rise above the dry surrounding plains. The Sierra Nevada range of California is a block that is 400 miles long and 80 miles wide. It was raised along a break in the surface of eastern California. Its highest part is near this eastern edge, and the block slopes gently westward.

Volcanic mountains are built of lava, ash, and cinders poured out from within the earth. The usual volcano is cone-shaped with a large hole, or crater, at the top. Among the famous volcanic peaks of the world are Fujiyama in Japan, Vesuvius in Italy, Popocatepetl and Orizaba in Mexico, El Misti in Peru, Aconcagua in

View from the top of Mount Everest.

The Bettmann Archive

Argentina, and the following six volcanic peaks in the United States: Mount Shasta in California, Mount Hood in Oregon, Mount Rainier in Washington, Katmai in Alaska, Kilauea and Mauna Loa in Hawaii.

Many mountain ranges have been formed by more than one of the ways described. In the Rockies of the United States are mountains made by folding, faulting, doming, and even the erosion of lavas. Some mountains, like the Catskills of New York, have been formed by the erosion of plateaus or level land raised high above the nearby countryside.

Young and Old Mountains

When first uplifted or built to great heights, mountains are young. Slopes are steep, streams are swift, and deep canyons may be rapidly eroded. Examples are the Alps, Himalayas, and Andes. But as years go by, mountain making stops and the wearing away goes on. Gradually the range is worn down. When the range is worn down to medium height, with broad open valleys, it is mature. Good examples are the Great Smokies of North Carolina and the White Mountains of New Hampshire. Eventually the mature range is worn down into low rolling hills—the old age of mountain history. The Laurentide Mountains of Canada, the Adirondacks of New York, and the Berkshire Hills of New England are old mountains, which have little of their once great height left.

Effects of Mountains on People

Mountains affect people in many ways. Some are great sources of mineral wealth. Mountains cause heavy rain or snow on the slopes that face the wind. The air that crosses them has to rise and thus cool. As it cools, moisture turns to rain. Rain of this kind is very important in California and other western states that depend on it for irrigation and other uses. In contrast, the side of the range away from the wind may be dry. An example is Reno, Nevada, near the east foot of the Sierra Nevada range, which receives less than 8 inches of rain per year.

Mountains also serve as barriers to human beings, and in this way they have made history. Rome's long leadership as a center of civilization and culture was due in part to the Alps. They saved Italy from invasion by barbarians from the north. Switzerland's long history of peace and independence is partly the result of its mountain position. In North America the low barrier of the Appalachians helped separate the English colonies along the seacoast from hostile Spanish colonies along the Mississippi. In later years, the Rockies were a much greater barrier between eastern United States and California. Transcontinental highways and railroads cross the Rockies by high passes or tunnels. Because mountain ranges are barriers to people, they serve much better than rivers as political boundaries.

From *Britannica Junior Encyclopaedia.*

Where is "the top of the world"? The world's highest mountain is Mount Everest in the Himalayas. In 1953 Sir Edmund Hillary and Tenzing Norgay struggled to reach its top. As you read the following selection, imagine you are along on their climb to "the top of the world."

To the Top of the World:
Sir Edmund Hillary and the Conquest of Everest

The Objective

On the morning of May 28, 1953, the wind banged out of the couloir, a great gully of snow below the southeast ridge of Mount Everest, shrieking, scouring new snow off hard green ice and dirty boulders a thousand feet down to Camp VIII on the South Col.[1]

At 8:45 A.M., the three-man support party left their wind-riddled tent at Camp VIII and started up from 26,000 feet. An hour later, the assault team, Edmund Hillary and Tenzing Norgay, began climbing, feeling the drag of altitude despite their oxygen. But the stumbling weakness quickly left their legs and they settled into a slow, rhythmic pace, making good progress, their crampons[2] biting into the glaring ice.

---

1. col: a pass between mountains or the low point of a ridge.
2. crampons: climbing spikes that attach to the soles of boots.

Hillary searched the face of the couloir for the support party. High above, like ants on a whitewashed wall, they were passing between leaping rock bluffs, hacking steps in the firm, fresh snow to make the ascent easier for Hillary and Tenzing and to help them conserve their strength and oxygen. Two days before, another assault team had climbed to 28,700 feet from the South Col in one day, the highest point ever reached by man, but were forced to turn back because of exhaustion and problems with their oxygen supply. On this second attempt, the expedition strategy was to establish a high camp on the southeast ridge. From there, the assault team would jump off and strike for the summit the following day.

Hillary shifted his gaze upward, searching for the crest of Everest. From afar, he remembered, the mountain looked like a hunchbacked Atlas[3] shoring up the sky of Tibet. Now, only a few thousand feet from the top, he saw its last shadowed pyramid, a floating, contorted right-hand curve, the summit held and hidden by ridges and a streaming plume of snow-mist.

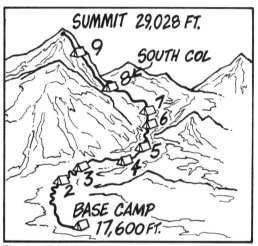

The expedition establishes and maintains camps up the side of Mt. Everest.

The assault team kicked up a steep ice face and hit the zigzag steps cut into the couloir. Their heavy packs and the spiking wind almost spilled them down the immense slope, and they hunched forward and fought to gain purchase with ice axes. They were gaining height, but their pace was sluggish, all sense of time distorted. The pair rested every thirty or forty steps, kneeling to ease the strain on their hearts and lungs.

For the first time, Hillary, a tough, lanky, hatchet-faced New Zealander, one of the greatest of a new generation of climbers, began to doubt that they'd make it to the summit. They were carrying too much weight in thin, bitter, deadly air that sapped a man's will

---

3. Atlas: giant in Greek mythology who is forced to support the heavens on his shoulders.

to go on and made his nerves, muscles, and mind deteriorate. Hillary knew their energy and endurance were draining too fast. Each man in the support party carried about forty-one pounds. He

The Bettmann Archive

and Tenzing—with sleeping bags, air mattresses, extra clothing, food, camera, and oxygen cylinders—closer to fifty. And above 27,000 feet were supplies cached[4] a few days before by John Hunt, the expedition leader, that had to be lifted to the camp on the southeast ridge.

Earlier that morning at Camp VIII, waking from a fitful sleep on oxygen, wretched from the wind and cold that had battered the tents all night, they discovered they'd have to start shorthanded. Two of the three Sherpa porters[5] with the support party were violently sick and went down the mountain. Hillary silently cursed them and felt no guilt. It was too high for pity; too much was at stake in the next hours after months of planning, hardship, and sacrifice. Everything had been timed to bring the right men to the right place in the right condition at the right time for the assault. One attack on the bastion[6] of Everest had been beaten back. Now Hillary and Tenzing were poised for a second. There would be no third chance.

Everest could be climbed at only two brief periods during the year—an approximate two-week lull in late spring between the monstrous northwest gales and the monsoon[7] that slammed in with wild snowstorms and avalanches, a shorter period in autumn considered too treacherous by most veteran mountaineers.

---

4. **cached:** hidden.
5. **Sherpa porters:** people who live on the slopes of the Himalayas and help carry supplies for mountain climbers.
6. **bastion:** stronghold.
7. **monsoon:** seasonal wind of southern Asia and the Indian Ocean.

With the two Sherpas gone, Hillary had to make a fast decision. There was no time to wait for fresh porters. He knew the weather could break momentarily and sweep them off the mountain. They could go back or redistribute the loads and carry the extra weight to the site of the high camp—gambling that the howling monsoon snows would hold another few days.

He glanced at Tenzing, a small, gravely handsome man. In twenty years the magnificent Sherpa had been on six Everest expeditions as porter and climber, and the year before had gone to within 787 feet of the top with the Swiss. He was thirty-nine years old and this was his last attempt. But there was no sentimentality in Hillary, no self-betrayal with false motives. When he made

Tenzing stands on top of the world's highest mountain.

Wide World Photos

the decision to go on, it was because of his own ego and confidence, his passion to be the first to conquer Everest . . . the same obsession that had haunted adventurers for years and killed sixteen.

From *To the Top of the World,* by Mark Sufrin.

In the nearly 40 years since Hillary and Tenzing conquered Mt. Everest, hundreds of climbers have reached the mountain's top. The following selection reveals the effects of human traffic on Everest's ecology.

Traffic, Trash Come to Everest

By Binaya Gurnacharya
The Associated Press

Traffic jams and landfills have come to Mount Everest, the roof of the world.

A growing number of nature lovers, and the flags, clothes, and oxygen tanks they leave behind, are turning parts of the majestic mountain into a garbage dump. And a crowded one at that.

A long line of climbers snaked near Everest's peak Thursday, vying for elbow room on the top. Americans, New Zealanders, Swiss, Soviets, Chinese, and Australians queued[1] up to reach the 29,028-foot summit.

ONE WAS the son of Sir Edmund Hillary, the first person to reach the summit. Hillary has expressed concern about damage to the fragile ecology of the Himalayas.

At least 17 people reached the crowded summit over the course of the day. Some came within minutes of each other. One group came from the north side, but the others hiked from the southeast, taking the traditional route made famous by Hillary, the New Zealander who first conquered Everest with his Nepalese guide, Tenzing Norgay, on May 29, 1953.

Fortunately, Thursday's climbers did not all reach the summit at once. Everest's pointy peak has room for only about 10 hikers—backpacks and oxygen gear included.

It has been one of the mountain's busiest seasons.

A Japanese team of three even tried to fly over Everest, in the first attempt to buzz the peak in a hot air balloon. They crashed Wednesday and one man suffered leg injuries.

IN LATE April, the Nepalese Tourist Administration said more than 100 people were climbing the mountain from the Nepalese side. Add to that a group of 30 climbers from a "peace group" of Soviets, Chinese, and Americans, who attacked the mountain from Tibet.

This mountainous traffic jam raises questions about the effects such hikes have on the ecology of Everest and the pristine[2] Himalayas. The mountain range, famed for its breathtaking views, pure air, and fertile valleys, is being ravaged[3] by deforestation.

Population increases in the Himalayan valleys have led farmers to cut down local forests for fuel and housing. Maneka Gandhi, India's minister of state for environment, warns that deforestation will have disastrous results far beyond the highlands. Already, it contributes to flooding in Bangladesh and erosion in the Indian plains.

Everest itself has been turned into a dump in some places—littered with mountaineers' used oxygen tanks, metal food containers, flags, and clothes.

---

1. queued: lined.

2. pristine: pure and unspoiled.

3. ravaged: damaged severely.

Unit 2: History

the study of past events

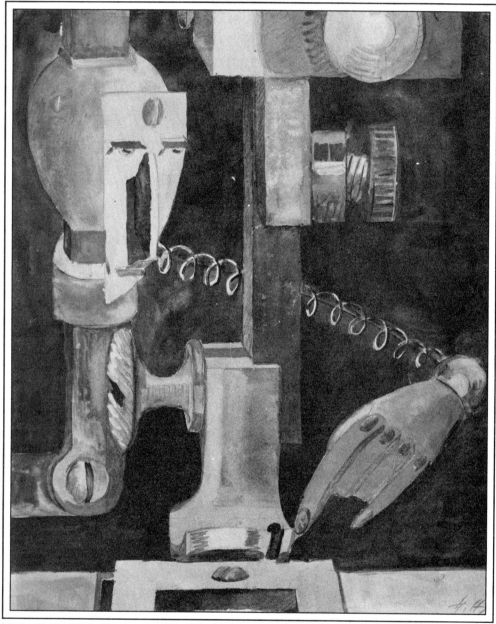

MAN AND MACHINE, 1921, Hannah Höch, Collection, The Museum of Modern Art, New York.
The Joan and Lester Avnet Collection.

What machines are important to you? Imagine your life without the machines you use at home or at work. Before the Industrial Revolution, life was very different. Read the following selection to find out how inventions and new methods of production changed people's lives.

The Industrial Revolution

The Industrial Revolution began the modern world. It began the world we live in today and our way of life in that world.

It is called a revolution because the changes it made were so great. These changes were also sudden, although the preparation for them took many years. It is called industrial because it had to do with manufacture. *Manufacture* means the making of every kind of article, from cotton cloth to brass pins.

The changes in the way these things were made changed the entire life of the people. They completely changed the habits of the workers—the men and women who produced the goods. They brought down prices, so that people were able to buy things they could not buy before. They made some men rich, but they reduced the earning power of others. They gave work to many who had been unemployed. At the same time, they took jobs away from many skilled workers.

The changes brought about by the Industrial Revolution at first caused tragedies. The principal change was the sudden introduction of machines powered by waterwheels or steam engines. This meant that manufacture had to be done in hot, crowded factories. It could no longer be done in comfortable homes—with spinning wheels, for example, or hand looms. Furthermore, the machines in the factories could be operated by completely unskilled labor. Children as young as six years old were set to work and kept at it for more than 12 hours a day.

These and a number of other bad practices were common for years. Then the law caught up with factory owners, and the tragic conditions were improved. This is the way with all revolutions. Very sudden changes always cause trouble until people get used to new ways. Reformers (those who wish to improve conditions) also must have time to bring order into new ways of life.

THE MORNING BELL, 1866, Winslow Homer, Yale University Art Gallery, Bequest of Stephen Carlton Clark, B.A. 1903.

WHERE IT BEGAN AND WHY

The Industrial Revolution began in England in the middle of the 18th century. This was about the time the English throne passed from George II to George III. It was in full swing at the time of the American Declaration of Independence in 1776.

It is true that there had been more and better manufacture on the continent of Europe than in England. In fact, the English had imported most of the manufactured goods they used.

In England farming and shipping had been the main occupations. Shipping had been particularly profitable during the 16th century. It was then the custom for the masters of English ships to attack and rob Spanish vessels coming from the Americas laden with gold. This gold had built up world trade, and many wealthy Englishmen were ready for new commercial ventures.

On the other hand, farming had become less important. The small farms had been taken into large landholdings. A great many farm workers were thrown out of their jobs. So there was much unemployed labor that could be put to work when the Industrial Revolution came.

Economists and political thinkers were concerned with the condition the country was in. They thought it would be a fine thing if England could devote herself to manufacturing and get her food and raw materials from her colonies abroad.

COTTAGE INDUSTRIES

Meanwhile, there was one industry that had grown up in England and was becoming increasingly prosperous. This was the spinning of cotton fiber into thread, by repeated twisting together of the fibers, and the weaving of cotton cloth. Because the spinners and weavers worked in their own homes, the making of cotton cloth was known as a *cottage industry.*

In some cottages there were spinning wheels and in others, hand looms. The spinning was done by women and the weaving was done by men. Agents would collect the thread as it was spun. They would take it to the weavers who would put it on the loom and weave it into cloth. The agents would then collect the cloth and take it to market. Generally the hand spinning was slower than the hand weaving. This meant that the weavers were idle much of the time.

The life of the workers in the cottage industries was a pleasant one, at least in comparison with what followed. The boss was like the father of a family and was generally kind. The cottage was in the country, with plenty of fresh air. Probably there was a kitchen garden, a pig pen, and a cow barn.

The workers' hours were their own. But when spinning fell far behind the weaving, there was more pressure, and the spinners had to work harder.

THE WAVE OF INVENTION

The start of the great change we call the Industrial Revolution came with improvements in weaving looms.

The operation of the loom was done entirely by hand. It was a slow operation until 1733, when an Englishman named John Kay patented the "flying shuttle."[1] The invention of the flying shuttle meant that the spinners had a harder time than ever trying to keep the weavers supplied with enough yarn.

One day in 1764, so the story goes, a clever Englishman named James Hargreaves sat watching his daughter at her spinning wheel. As she stood up to rest from her work, the wheel accidentally tipped over and lay on its side. Hargreaves watched the wheel and spindle still turning. Like a flash, an idea came to him.

He lost no time in constructing a spinning machine in which eight spindles could be turned at once. He tried it. It worked. Remembering the accident that had given him the idea, he named his new invention the "jenny," after his daughter.

The wave of invention had started to roll. New things were being done all over England. Canals were being dug, new mining machinery was being installed, and sawmills were operating. There were even railroads, although the cars on them were drawn by horses. Everywhere there was a new interest in scientific discoveries.

THE FIRST "PRIME MOVERS"

In this atmosphere of change, it was understandable that inventors should think up machines for applying power to both spinning and weaving. But where was that power to come from? Manpower and animal power had done most of the work of the world for thousands of years. They were not enough. There had to be ways of harnessing the forces of nature—the *prime movers*—to machinery so as to make it run without human effort.

Waterpower

This had already been done with water in the rivers. In the swift streams of the European continent, waterwheels had been made to turn many sorts

---

1. **flying shuttle:** a device that uses a spring to shoot a thread back and forth between the threads that run lengthwise on a weaving loom.

of mills for wood and iron work. In England water-powered gristmills, or flour mills, were common. Why not hitch a waterwheel to the new spinning and weaving inventions?

The task of doing this was undertaken by Richard Arkwright, who was not so much an inventor himself as a combiner of other men's inventions. Arkwright has been rightly called the "father of the factory system." He began by putting the English textile industry—the making of cloth—into factories that were run by waterpower.

Before Arkwright there was nothing that could really be called a factory. A *factory* is a place where workers and machinery are all together under one roof. Factories speeded up manufacture to an astonishing degree.

Coal and Iron

England had two great resources that made important contributions to the Industrial Revolution. This, indeed, was one of the reasons why the revolution took place there. These resources were coal and iron. Iron was melted down to be made into tools, weapons, utensils, axles, and so on. Coal was burned as fuel.

Steam

Inventors came thick and fast in the 18th century. As a boy, Thomas Newcomen was fascinated by boiling water and by the steam that came with such force from the spout of the kettle. When he grew to manhood, he was able to make an engine that worked. Newcomen is hailed as one of the great inventors of history because he started the practical use of steam power.

Steam Changes the Factory Geography

By the late 1700s, James Watt, a Scotsman, had perfected a steam engine very different from Newcomen's. He was assisted by a scientist named Joseph Black and a businessman named Matthew Boulton.

As soon as the engines made by Boulton and Watt were tried in the textile factories, it was obvious that they were far better than the waterwheels. No longer did the mills have to be built close to a stream or river. They could operate anywhere. They were set up, then, in the cities rather than in rural districts. In the cities the labor supply was more plentiful. The workers could live at home and go every day to the mill. They did not have to be housed in dormitories, as they had been when they had to work far from home.

By this time the textile factories were much larger. Here, too, there were power looms. Everything from the raw cotton to the finished cloth could be made in one place. This worked a great hardship on the cottage weavers, who were now crowded into dark, hot factory rooms.

WORKING CONDITIONS BECOME HARDER

With the introduction of steam, the work became harder for the workers. The textile factories became hotter and damper than ever. The hours were just as long. Women and children were still employed to tend the machines. The poorly paid workers lived around the factories in crowded, dirty, and unsanitary districts of a town or city.

By the end of the 18th century reformers in England had already begun to expose the bad conditions in the industrial towns. Bills (drafts of suggested laws) were being introduced in the Parliament to limit the hours and to forbid the employment of very young children.

When the 19th century dawned, the writers took a hand. Authors like Thomas Carlyle, Charles Dickens, and George Eliot wrote books about the sufferings of the factory workers. These accounts were so moving that the whole English public became aroused. Some employers, such as Robert Peel, Robert Owen, and John Fielden, tried to improve conditions in the factories they owned. But this was difficult to do.

The factory system had laid such a hold on English industrialists that one employer could not raise wages or shorten hours unless all employers did. Competition was fierce. If a kind industrialist put through expensive reforms, it increased the prices of his cloth or yarn. He would be undersold and put out of business by a greedy man who did not try to improve conditions. But when the law stepped in, all employers were forced to change their ways.

SOCIAL EFFECTS

It is easy to see how the Industrial Revolution changed more than the factory geography of England. It changed the living habits and economic conditions of almost all the English people as well. Families everywhere moved to the cities to get employment. Country villages were deserted. The cities grew by leaps and bounds. Now that waterpower was no longer necessary, towns grew up far from rivers.

Under the new industrial ownership men grew enormously rich in a short time. When labor was paid almost starvation wages, there was an immense gap between the rich and the poor.

The nation was no longer self-supporting in food as agriculture became less important. More and more food, raw cotton, bar iron, flax, and other raw materials were imported. All the time the British Empire grew in size and activity.

After Britain lost the American colonies, it tried to keep the United States agricultural and to prevent it from becoming industrial. Parliament made laws that did not allow English machines to be sold to Americans. Laws even forbade English inventors and artisans to migrate to the new American states.

THE INDUSTRIAL REVOLUTION IN AMERICA

The Industrial Revolution took a long time to cross the Atlantic. Americans were too busy exploring and settling the West to devote much time to invention and the making of machines. American women were still using the old-fashioned spinning wheel long after yarn was being spun by machines in England.

The factory system came to America from England. It was first introduced by an English textile worker named Samuel Slater. He realized that a fortune could be made by the person who introduced cotton manufacture to Americans. Slater disguised himself to avoid being caught under the new English laws. In 1789 he arrived in New York with all the knowledge of English textile machinery in his head. Sam Slater had a remarkable memory. When he got to Pawtucket, Rhode Island, he was able to build a whole factory of machines that could spin as fast and as well as those assembled by Arkwright in England.

But Slater was a kind man. He was determined from the start that there should never be such horrible conditions in his Rhode Island mills as were common in England even then (1791).

For a long time the only power used for manufacture in the United States was waterpower. This was because steam engines, when they were built in America, were used entirely for transportation. Transportation was the great American need. The country was so large that to explore and settle it quickly, steamboats and railroads were urgently needed. Thus it was not until about the time of the American Civil War (the 1860s) that steam-operated factories became common.

The first American industrial revolution did not produce the suffering and abuses of the English one. This was because there was endless opportunity for everyone in the new, unsettled country. Also, for almost a century farming was the occupation most Americans favored. This was true especially in the rich soil of the West.

In the last quarter of the 19th century the United States became thoroughly industrialized. It soon came to lead the world in machine manufacture. At the close of the century, labor suffered from the eagerness

The American colonies resist England.

The Bettmann Archive

Children work in a cotton mill.

of employers to make money even at the expense of their employees. In later years conditions improved. Labor unions were formed to look out for the interests of the workers. American industrialists also made many changes that would benefit their employees.

It is interesting to realize that the growth of the factory system and machine production in the United States started from conditions exactly the opposite of those that had existed a century earlier in England. In England many thousands were unemployed, so they could be brought into the new factory system. But in the United States there was a labor shortage because everyone wanted to be a farmer in the West. The farmers had to be supplied with manufactured goods—cloth, tools, firearms, utensils, shoes, pottery, paper. This meant that the factories in the East had to have as many automatic machines as possible. These were machines that could turn out goods by mass production. In other words, they could produce the greatest quantity of goods with the least possible human labor.

From *The New Book of Knowledge.*

What would you do if you needed uniforms for thousands of soldiers and each uniform had to be made by hand? In 1861, at the outbreak of the Civil War, most people made their own clothes. Read to find out how today's clothing industry began.

TAILOR, 1940, William Gropper, Hirschhorn Museum and Sculpture Garden, Smithsonian Institution, Gift of Joseph H. Hirshhorn, 1966.

A Democracy of Clothing

At the outbreak of the Civil War in 1861, the government had to provide hundreds of thousands of uniforms for men in the army. This was the first time in American history that so much clothing had been required all at once. During the American Revolution the colonial army had been relatively small, and most soldiers brought along their own clothing. In the later wars too—the War of 1812 and the Mexican War—the armies were only a few thousand strong.

So in 1861 there was no large ready-made[1] clothing industry. The simple explanation was that it had always been the custom for each family to make its own clothes. Just as the meals that American families eat today are usually made at home, so it used to be with coats, suits, socks, and nearly everything else a person wore. Only the rich few, who could afford to look elegant, would hire a skilled tailor.

In New England in the early nineteenth century, there were a few shops that sold ready-made clothing. But these offered only the cheapest grades. In New Bedford, Massachusetts, for example, sailors who had just returned from a three-year whaling voyage needed new clothing quickly.

---

1. ready-made: made beforehand for general sale.

Other sailors who had just signed on for a new voyage hastily had to collect supplies for their months at sea. The stores that sold them their clothing were called "slopshops" because the clothing they sold was "slops," an Old Norse word for the wide-bottomed trousers that sailors wore. Slopshop clothing was of poor quality, and the customer did not expect a good fit.

In the South, too, some plantation owners bought cheap ready-made clothing for their slaves. In Western mining towns the men who had quickly joined the Gold Rush had usually left their families behind. There were too few women to provide homemade clothing and not enough rich people to support a tailor. Miners had to go to a store. "Store-boughten" clothing was better than nothing.

People took it for granted that if you bought ready-made clothing from a store, it could not possibly fit you well. They believed that everybody was quite a different size. Therefore, they said the only way to make clothing fit was to have it made specially (either at home or by a tailor) to your very own measurements. How could a manufacturer possibly turn out thousands of suits, each a different size, for thousands of different people? A suit you bought in a store would surely be too loose in some places and too tight in others. Manufacturers—without even trying—had given up the effort to provide sizes that would really fit.

Take shoes, for example. Before the mid-nineteenth century, even after shoemaking machinery had been invented, the shoes you could buy ready-made in a store were usually "straights." That meant there was actually no difference between the shoe sold for the right foot and the shoe sold for the left foot. If you really wanted your shoes to fit, you had to hire a shoemaker to make a pair especially for you.

The uniform makers in the Civil War learned a lesson. They found that if they made quite a few different sizes they could provide almost everybody with a reasonably good fit. They noticed that certain combinations of measurements were more common than others. For example, lots of men with a 36-inch waist also had a 30-inch trouser length. They kept track of the sizes of the uniforms they made.

When the Civil War was over in 1865 and hundreds of thousands of veterans suddenly needed civilian clothes, the United States actually had a clothing industry. Manufacturers had learned so much about the commonest measurements of the human body that they could produce ready-made suits which fitted better than most homemade suits and almost as well as the best tailor-made suits. Merchants now began to open clothing stores for everybody because their assortments of sizes would fit any customer. Americans of all classes and occupations were glad to buy their suits ready-made.

The age of statistics—a new age of careful measurement—had arrived in the world of clothing. In 1880 a statistically-minded tailor named Daniel Edward Ryan, after years of collecting facts, published *Human Proportions in Growth: Being the*

Complete Measurement of the Human Body for Every Age and Size during the Years of Juvenile Growth. The new "science of sizes" gave clothing manufacturers a scientific guide for customers of all ages.

A family sews garments by hand.

To put this new science to use and to stock clothing stores with all the different sizes, there had to be a whole factory full of new machinery. The old tedious way of making garments —cutting cloth for one suit at a time and then sewing each seam by hand—was not good enough.

Most of the labor went into sewing. So the most important new machine would be a sewing machine. In 1831 a Paris tailor had made a workable sewing machine and had begun to use it making uniforms for the French army. But Paris tailors, afraid that they would lose their jobs, smashed the machines and drove the inventor out of the city. Soon afterward, several Americans made sewing machines.

Walter Hunt was one of the most ingenious inventors of the age. Once when he needed money to pay a debt, within the space of only three hours he invented the safety pin, made a model of it, and sold the idea for $400. But he was more interested in making inventions than in making money. Among his new devices were a knife sharpener, a stove

to burn hard coal, an ice plow, a repeating rifle, a street-sweeping machine, and paper collars. By 1832 Hunt had perfected a machine that sewed a lockstitch that would not unravel. But Hunt was not a businessman, and he did not even bother to patent[2] his invention.

A few years later Elias Howe, who had been raised on a Massachusetts farm and then worked as apprentice to a scientific instrument maker in Cambridge, made the same invention on his own. He patented his machine in 1846.

To prove that his machine really worked, Howe staged a public sewing race at the Quincy Hall Clothing Manufactory in Boston. He challenged five of the speediest seamstresses. Ten seams of equal length were prepared. One was given to each seamstress, and

---

2. patent: obtain an official document that protects an inventor's rights to make, use, or sell an invention.

five were given to Howe at his machine. To everybody's amazement, before any of the seamstresses had finished her one seam, Howe had finished his five. His sewing machine was declared the winner.

But people feared that the sewing machine would put needy seamstresses out of work. As late as 1849 the sewing machine was still so rare that a man carried one around western New York State charging an admission fee of 12 1/2 cents to see "A Great Curiosity!! The Yankee Sewing-Machine." Ladies took specimens of machine sewing home to show their friends.

Not for long would machine sewing remain a curiosity. A remarkable go-getting salesman and organizer had become interested in it. When Isaac Merrit Singer saw his first sewing machine in 1850 his main aim—like that of Henry Ford after him—was to make machines so cheap that he could sell them by the hundreds of thousands. When he used Howe's patented designs without permission, the courts eventually made him pay for the right to use them. But in 1856 Singer persuaded Howe to join a great "Sewing Machine Combination" to make machines with all the latest improvements.

Singer's dream came true, for by 1871 more than a half-million sewing machines were being manufactured each year. The combination of Howe design and Singer salesmanship sent American sewing machines all over the world. "Every nook and corner of Europe," the advertisements boasted, "knows the song of this tireless Singer."

Sewing machines helped workers sew the seams of clothing faster. Next to sewing the seams, what took the most time in making a man's coat or suit was cutting the cloth to the pattern. To cut heavy cloth for one suit at a time was tedious. But it was hard to make a knife that would cut through thick piles of cloth. The knife tended to twist the cloth so that the bottom pieces came out a different shape. This problem was solved in the 1870s when new high-speed, steam-powered cutting machines sliced neatly through twenty or more thicknesses. In the 1880s a Boston inventor perfected the machine that saved more hours by automatically cutting and finishing buttonholes.

Each factory-produced suit had to be neatly pressed. But the old heavy pressing iron (called a "goose" because it was so large and had a long awkward handle) was slow. A clever apprentice, Adon J. Hoffman, who was using a "goose" in a tailor shop in Syracuse, New York, dislocated his shoulder so that he could not handle the cumbersome iron. So he invented a presser he could operate with his feet. A foot pedal controlled the steam pressure that pushed down the top pad. All the operator had to do with his hands was to lay the garment between the pads. Within a few years Hoffman had become rich by selling thousands of his new steam pressers.

As the population grew and the American worker prospered, the demand for good ready-made clothing went up. At the same time, too, near the end of the nineteenth century, the flood of immigrants from Germany, Russia, and Poland included many who had been tailors over there. They naturally went to work in clothing factories here. But the new sewing machine was making the tailor's skills less needed than ever. In the new clothing factories, the wives and children of these immigrants found quick employment.

Some of these factories became "sweatshops," where women and children worked long hours in stuffy rooms for low wages. But soon new laws required the children to stay in school. Meanwhile labor unions, led by enterprising[3] immigrants, organized the clothing workers to demand better wages and shorter hours. Eventually the unions themselves would become rich enough to provide hospitals, clubhouses, and scholarships for their members.

By the end of the nineteenth century the United States saw a revolution in clothing. Here, for the first time in history, there was the beginning of a democracy of clothing. Here you did not have to be rich to dress well. A new industry was finding ways to make a stylish suit that any man could afford. Before 1900, nine-tenths of the men and boys in the United States were wearing ready-made clothing that they had bought in a store. Even the rich who once hired a tailor found a ready-made suit to fit. Americans dressed more like one another than people in any Old World nation. The new immigrant could go into a clothing store and buy a ready-made outfit that made him an instant American.

Levi Strauss & Co. advertises pants in the late 1800s.

---

3. **enterprising:** energetic and daring.

From *The Landmark History of the American People*, by Daniel J. Boorstin.

Many people stood in line to get jobs in factories that sprang up in the late 1800s and early 1900s. Sadie Frowne, a 17-year-old woman who came from Poland to America, went to work in a shirt factory. Read the following paragraphs to discover how she felt about her work.

In Her Own Words: A Factory Worker

I went to work in what is called a factory. I made shirts by machine. I was new at the work and the boss scolded me a great deal.

The factory is in the third floor of a brick building. It is twenty feet long and fourteen feet wide. There are fourteen machines in it. I get up at half past five every morning. I have a cup of coffee, a bit of bread and then go to work. Often I get to the factory at six o'clock.

The machines go like mad all day. Sometimes in my haste I get my finger caught and the needle goes right through it. It goes so quick that it does not hurt much. I bind the finger up with a piece of cotton and go on working. We all have accidents like that.

While we work the boss walks around checking the finished shirts. He makes us do them over again if they are not right. But I am getting good at the work. By next year I will be making seven dollars a week. The machines are run by foot power. At the end of the day I feel so weak that I could just lie down and sleep.

But I am going back to night school again this winter. Plenty of my friends go there. Like me, they did not have a chance to learn anything in the old country. It is good to have an education. It makes you feel higher.

Adapted from "The Story of a Sweatshop Girl," *The Independent,* 1902.

This poem dates back to the 1800s, when many young women worked long hours in hot, crowded factories. Read to discover how work in a factory changed one little girl's life.

The Little Factory Girl
to a More Fortunate Playmate

I often think how once we used in summer fields to play,
And run about and breathe the air that made us glad and gay;
We used to gather buttercups, and chase the butterfly—
I loved to feel the light breeze lift my hair as it went by!

5 Do you still play in those bright fields? and are the flowers
      still there?
There are no fields where I live now—no flowers any where!
But day by day I go and turn a dull and tedious wheel,
You cannot think how sad, and tired, and faint I often feel.

I hurry home to snatch the meal my mother can supply,
10 Then back to hasten to the task—that not to hate I try,
At night my mother kisses me, when she has combed my hair,
And laid me in my little bed, but—I'm not happy there—

I dream about the factory, the fines that on us wait—
I start and ask my father if—I have not lain too late?
15 And once I heard him sob and say—"Oh better were a grave,
Than such a life as this for thee, thou little sinless slave!"

I wonder if I ever shall obtain a holiday?
Oh if I do, I'll go to you, and spend it all in play.
And then I'll bring some flowers, if you will give me some;
20 And at my work I'll think of them and holidays to come!

The Bettmann Archive

From The Man, May 13, 1834.

In 1723 a 17-year-old left his home in Boston to seek his fortune in Philadelphia. Over the years the young man met success as a printer, author, scientist, inventor, patriot, and diplomat. Read the following selection to find out more about this remarkable person.

Poor Richard

Colonial America Produces a Genius, 1706-1790

The rain pounded against the roof of the old inn. Young Ben Franklin, soaked to the skin and shivering against the drafts of raw October wind that sifted through the walls, wished that he had never run away. No wonder people stared at him suspiciously—he cut a miserable figure with only his working clothes to wear; his trunk had been sent by sea. His entire wealth consisted of a Dutch dollar and a copper shilling.

Hungry and cold, Ben decided to keep to his room to avoid questions that his seventeen-year-old mind might find difficult to answer. Another day should bring him to Burlington, New Jersey, where he could catch the boat to Philadelphia. Suddenly his sense of humor made him see the other side of the situation. If he felt distracted, imagine the bewilderment he must have left in Boston!

The boy flung himself on the bed, drawing up his knees and trying to absorb a little cheer from the warmth of his body. Events in an already busy life flashed across his mind, and from habit he sorted them into logical order.

First he had been born—a hard fact to dispute insofar as there were fourteen brothers and sisters in the Franklin family to vouchsafe[1] for his arrival in Boston on January 17, 1706. There had been talk of making a clergyman of him, but after one year of school Ben's father had abandoned that notion. Education was one extravagance Josiah Franklin couldn't afford. He now had two more children, making a total of seventeen.

Ben had not felt greatly dismayed at giving up his formal schooling. He could teach himself, and he believed he had been born with the ability to read, for he couldn't remember the time when the printed page had been any mystery to him. Bunyan's *Pilgrim's Progress,* the books of Daniel Defoe, Plutarch's *Lives,* Burton's *Historical Collections,* Cotton Mather's *Essay to do Good* were books over which he had pored till he knew large portions by memory.

Ben's real ambition had been to go to sea, but this scheme his father had sternly opposed. Instead, Ben found himself helping his father as a tallow-chandler[2] and soap-boiler. Nothing in the trade of cutting wick for candles, filling the dipping molds, attending the shop or running errands had appealed to him. Even Josiah Franklin admitted that Ben was a poor hand at the craft, and so at the age of twelve the boy was apprenticed to his printer brother James.

James proved too strict the master, too ready to whip the rebellious spirit out of Ben. Of all the tricks Ben played, James resented most the articles Ben wrote under the assumed name of "Mrs. Silence Dogood." In James's newspaper, *New England Courant,* these articles appeared until one day Ben inadvertently divulged[3] his secret. For the next few moments the roof all but blew off the Boston print shop. Ben wasn't old enough to write anything worth space in the *Courant!* If ever the young whippersnapper deserved a caning,[4] this deceit was the perfect example.

Ben's rebel heart had known then that his parting with James was only a question of time. He remained while James served a short prison

1. **vouchsafe:** provide evidence.
2. **tallow-chandler:** candlemaker.
3. **inadvertently divulged:** accidentally told.
4. **caning:** beating.

term for printing satirical[5] pieces in the *Courant* that offended the Crown's authorities, but soon afterward the breaking point came. So here he was, hearing the rain pound the roof, and wondering if he had jumped from the frying pan into the fire.

In another day Ben reached Burlington and the next morning Philadelphia. His wealth now was reduced to the single Dutch dollar, but his hunger had become so unbearable that he stopped at the baker's and parted with three pennies for three large rolls. With a roll under each arm, leaving him free to eat the third, he walked jauntily[6] along Philadelphia's Market Street.

A young girl, standing at the door of one of the houses, turned and laughed at the ridiculous spectacle Ben made. Her name was Debby Read, and one day she would become Mrs. Benjamin Franklin, but at that moment nothing was further from Ben's mind than romance. Instead of letting the girl know that he noticed, he went on to a Quaker meeting, where, overcome by the fatigues of a long journey, he promptly fell asleep.

Thus began the independent career of one of the most remarkable persons Colonial America would produce. With a great knowledge of books and an easy flow of conversation, Ben soon became the warm friend of Sir William Keith, governor of the colony, who offered to set him up in the printing business. Ben traveled to England to buy the equipment for his shop, but the money Sir William had promised to send never reached London. An undaunted[7] Ben settled cheerfully into English life, supported himself as a printer, and after eighteen months financed his own voyage home to America. A year and a half after returning, he had established his own business and was busily publishing *The Pennsylvania Gazette*.

In 1732 there appeared in the book stalls a new publication—*Poor Richard's Almanack*. In a land where books were very scarce, almost every home in time seemed to contain two—the Bible and the latest *Poor Richard*. Franklin used the name of Richard Saunders to disguise his authorship, and the homely[8] advice Poor Richard gave spoke the common sense people needed to conquer a wilderness. "A penny saved is a penny earned," wrote Franklin, who had turned vegetarian so that the money he saved on food could be used to buy books. "Like cats in

---

5. satirical: sarcastic.
6. jauntily: light-heartedly.
7. undaunted: unafraid.
8. homely: plain or familiar.

airpumps, to subsist we strive," wrote Franklin, now one of the busiest men in America.

Poor Richard caught the spirit of the struggle for the settler fishing the waters off the Maine coast, for the farmer who left his plow to fight Indians, for the planter of tobacco in Tidewater, Virginia and the planter of rice in the Carolinas. Poor Richard was quoted by father to son, and by son to his son. Even today it is a rare boy or girl who does not hear advice originally published in *Poor Richard's Almanack:* "God helps them that help themselves." "Little strokes fell great oaks."

BENJAMIN FRANKLIN, Charles W. Peale, Philadelphia, Pennsylvania Historical Society.

"Early to bed and early to rise, makes a man healthy, wealthy, and wise."

For Franklin the days surely must have started early, and at times his neighbors must have wondered where next they would find him. One day he would be out in a thunderstorm, flying a kite to prove that lightning is electricity. Or he would be showing the lightning rod he had invented; or demonstrating the Franklin stove he had built, which began the stove industry in America; or the bifocal glasses he had designed; or the platform rocking chair that still can be found creaking in many American parlors.

"Debby," Franklin said to his wife, "I wish the good Lord had seen fit to make each day just twice as long as it is. Perhaps then I really could accomplish something."

So, handicapped by days that contained only twenty-four hours, Franklin organized the first fire department in Philadelphia, improved the city's police system, helped to organize the first hospital in America, reorganized the postal system in the colonies, founded an academy that became the University of Pennsylvania, started the first circulating library, and complained because he couldn't come back in a hundred years to see how things were working out.

From *The Rainbow Book of American History,* by Earl Schenck Miers.

Did you celebrate America's 200th birthday in 1976? In 1876 a great world's fair in Philadelphia marked the special occasion of the nation's first 100 years of freedom. As you read the following selection, note the achievements that were celebrated.

A Century ≈ of ≈ Freedom

In 1876 Americans looked back with pride on what had been achieved in the century that began with the signing of the Declaration of Independence. In 1776 the Republic had covered an area of 800,000 square miles. Now, only a hundred years later, the nation reached from ocean to ocean, and embraced an area of 3,500,000 square miles of land and water. The population of the colonies had been slightly more than 2,250,000. Now, almost 50,000,000 people lived under the Stars and Stripes.

Americans had many reasons to be proud. Agriculture had become a science. In 1776, cereals, potatoes, flax, and tobacco had been the chief products. In 1876 Americans raised every kind of agricultural product on more than 189,000,000 acres of improved farmland. American inventors had already greatly reduced the drudgery of farming. Cyrus Hall McCormick had given the farmer a machine to cut grain, and John E. Heath had perfected a machine that not only cut grain but also tied it into bundles. John F. Appleby was working on a threshing

The Statue of Liberty's torch is displayed at the Centennial Exposition.

The Bettmann Archive

machine that would separate the grain from the chaff as the farmer moved along his field. A hundred years ago many an American had plowed with little more than a crooked stick. Now, through the genius of Jethro Wood, the farmer used an iron plow with replaceable parts.

During the same century, an enormous amount of mineral wealth had been discovered—coal, copper, petroleum, gold, silver. The Marquette Range of northern Michigan had recently been found to have rich deposits of iron. Coal and iron were the basis of a growing steel industry. The oil wells of northwestern Pennsylvania were creating a new industry of incredible wealth. Lumbering in New England, Michigan, and Wisconsin was still another proof of America's great natural resources.

American Achievements

The growth of manufacturing in America had been enormous. Before the Revolution, Great Britain had discouraged any type of industry in order to keep the colonies dependent on the mother country. But once Americans could decide their own way of life, they had moved swiftly ahead. Patent-office records told a dramatic story of how American inventive genius was causing a boom in American industry. In the years from 1790 to 1800, a total of 306 patents was issued; from 1860 to 1870, the total was 79,612. The steamboat, the locomotive, the electromagnetic telegraph, and the sewing machine were all inventions perfected by Americans. Whatever could be made of iron, Americans manufactured. Business houses now carried their customers above the ground floor in the elevator invented by Elisha Graves Otis. Once no two watches in America had been alike, but now watches were manufactured with interchangeable parts, so that they could be turned out by mass production.

American ships, sailing every sea in the world, had increased the value of the nation's exports from $14,262,000 in 1770 to over $600,000,000 in 1875. Once inland travel in America had depended on the pack mule and the canoe, and now railroads and canals linked ocean with ocean. Steamboats had turned the Great Lakes into navigable inland seas.

Education, too, had thrived. In 1776 there had been few colleges in America. Now, a hundred years later, there were 349. The Morrill Act, passed in 1862, offered liberal grants of public land to help states build colleges teaching agriculture and mechanics. The public school population had grown considerably. People read more. In 1776 a printer could produce about 250 newspaper sheets an hour printed on one side; now Robert Hoe's steam-driven "power press" turned out 15,000 complete newspapers an hour, folded for delivery.

Centennial Exposition

To celebrate these achievements of a century of freedom, a great world's fair was planned. It was held in Philadelphia, where the Declaration of Independence had been signed. Opening in May and closing in November of 1876, the Centennial Exposition drew an attendance of 9,910,965 persons.

In the Main Exhibition Hall, covering twenty-one-and-a-half acres, they visited "the largest building in the world." Here more than thirty countries exhibited products of their science, invention, and industry. One third of the space was required to show the products of America.

In Machinery Hall, covering thirteen acres, they stood before a man-made waterfall thirty-six feet wide and thirty-

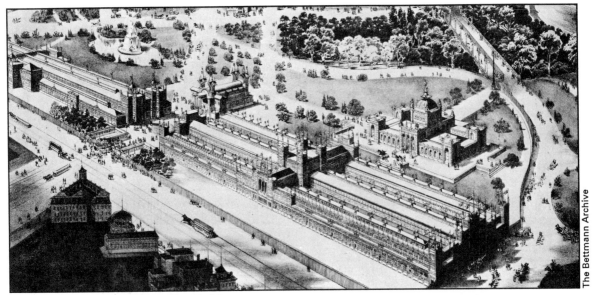

The Centennial Exposition's fairground and buildings.

three feet deep, over which 30,000 gallons of water poured every minute.

In Memorial Hall—also called the Fine Arts Building—they roamed 20,000 feet of floor space to gaze upon an exhibition of paintings and statuary. At the Horticultural Building, surrounded by thirty-five acres of gardens, they gaped at orange and lemon trees and at a century plant[1] about to bloom.

Then they went home—often in luxurious new Pullman cars[2] with a "Hotel Dining Car" and protected by the air brakes that George Westinghouse had invented in 1869. In New York City, they went home to Grand Central Station, completed in 1871, and to the elevated train that, drawn by small steam locomotives, carried passengers up Ninth Avenue.

They went home to the new sports that were now the American's passion—professional baseball, intercollegiate football (first played between Princeton and Rutgers in 1869), lawn tennis (imported from England)—and to such farm pastimes as the husking bee, where if a young man happened to find a red ear of corn, he was permitted to kiss any girl present. They went home to pore over the pages of a mail-order catalogue, the first of which was issued by Montgomery Ward & Company in 1873, and to use the typewriter that had been perfected that year.

It seemed that no country could be more wonderful than the one they lived in. They were sure that in the years to come America would be even more wonderful.

1. **century plant:** a desert plant once believed to bloom only every 100 years.
2. **Pullman cars:** comfortable railroad passenger cars for day or night travel.

From *The Golden Book of the History of the United States,* by Earl Schenck Miers.

Unit 3: Political Science

the study of how governments work

THE FOUR FREEDOMS, THE FREEDOM OF SPEECH, 1943, Norman Rockwell, Printed by permission of the Estate of Norman Rockwell, copyright © 1943 Estate of Norman Rockwell.

Woodcut of the Constitutional Convention in Philadelphia, 1787.

How easily can 55 people keep a secret? In 1787, over a period of 17 weeks, 55 men met in Philadelphia to decide on the best form of government for the United States. They wanted to keep their discussions secret because the men believed public debate would slow their progress. Read to find out about this fascinating event known as the Constitutional Convention.

Shh! We're Writing the Constitution

After the Revolutionary War most people in America were glad that they were no longer British. Still, they were not ready to call themselves Americans. The last thing they wanted was to become a nation. They were citizens of their own separate states, just as they had always been: each state different, each state proud of its own character, each state quick to poke fun at other states. To Southerners, New Englanders might be "no-account Yankees." To New Englanders, Pennsylvanians might be "lousy Buckskins." But to everyone the states themselves were all important. "Sovereign states," they called them. They loved the sound of "sovereign" because it meant that they were their own bosses.

George Washington, however, scoffed at the idea of "sovereign states." He knew that the states could not be truly independent for long and survive. Ever since the Declaration of Independence had been signed, people had referred to the country as the United States of America. It was about time, he thought, for them to act and feel unified.

Once during the war Washington had decided it would be a good idea if his troops swore allegiance to the United States. As a start, he lined up some troops from New Jersey and asked them to take such an oath. They looked at Washington as if he'd taken leave of his senses. How could they do that? they cried. New Jersey was their country.

So Washington dropped the idea. In time, he hoped, the states would see that they needed to become one nation, united under a strong central government.

But that time would be long in coming. For now, as they started out on their independence, the thirteen states were satisfied to be what they called a federation, a kind of voluntary league of states. In other words, each state legislature sent delegates to a Continental Congress which was supposed to act on matters of common concern.

In September 1774, when the First Continental Congress met, the common concern was Great Britain. Two years later, after the Declaration of Independence had been signed, the concern was that the country needed some kind of government. Not a fully developed government because of course they had their states. All they wanted were some basic rules to hold them together to do whatever needed to be done. So the Congress wrote the Articles of Confederation which outlined rules for a "firm league of friendship." In practice, however, the states did not always feel a firm need to follow any rules.

The Congress, for instance, could ask the states to contribute money to pay the country's debts, but if the states didn't feel like contributing, no one could make them. Congress could declare war but it couldn't fight unless the states felt like supplying soldiers. The trouble was that their president had no definite powers and the country had no overall legal system. So although the Congress could make all the rules it wanted, it couldn't enforce any of them. Much of the time the states didn't even bother to send delegates to the meetings.

By 1786, it was becoming obvious that changes were needed. People were in debt, a few states were printing paper money that was all but worthless, and in the midst of this disorder some people could see that America would fall apart if it didn't have a sound central government with power to act for all the states. George Washington, of course, was one who had felt strongly about this for a long time. Alexander Hamilton was another. Born and brought up in the Caribbean Islands, he had no patience with the idea of state loyalty. America was nothing but a monster with thirteen heads, he said. James Madison from Virginia wanted a strong America too. He was a little man, described as being "no bigger than a half a piece of soap," but he had big ideas for his country.

In 1786 these men, among others, suggested to the Congress that all the states send delegates to a Grand Convention in Philadelphia to improve the existing form of government. It sounded innocent. Just a matter of revising the old Articles of Confederation to make the government work better. No one would quarrel with that.

But they did.

Rhode Island refused to have anything to do with the convention. Patrick Henry, when asked to be a delegate from Virginia, said he "smelt a rat" and wouldn't go. Willie Jones of North Carolina didn't say what he smelled, but he wouldn't go either.

But in the end the convention was scheduled to meet in the State House in Philadelphia on May 14, 1787.

James (or "Jemmy") Madison was so worked up about it that he arrived from Virginia eleven days early. George Washington left his home, Mount Vernon, on May 9 with a headache and an upset stomach, but he arrived in Philadelphia on the night of May 13th. The next morning a few delegates from Pennsylvania and a few from Virginia came to the meeting but there needed to be seven states present to conduct business. Since there were only two, the meeting was adjourned.

The FEDERAL EDIFICE.

State House and Congress Hall in Philadelphia.

It was May 25th before delegates from enough states showed up. They blamed their delays on the weather, muddy roads, personal business, lack of money. Delegates from New Hampshire couldn't scrape up enough money to come until late July, but even so, they beat John Francis Mercer of Maryland. He sauntered into the State House on August 6th.

The most colorful arrival was that of Benjamin Franklin who at eighty-one was the oldest of the delegates. Because he experienced so much pain when he was bounced about in a carriage, Franklin came to the convention in a Chinese sedan chair carried by four prisoners from the Philadelphia jail. (He lived in the city so they didn't have far to carry him.)

In all, there would be fifty-five delegates, although coming and going as they did, there were seldom more than thirty there at the same time. The first thing the delegates did was to elect George Washington president of the convention. They escorted him to his official chair on a raised platform. Then the other members of the convention took their seats at tables draped with green woolen cloth. James Madison sat in the front of the room and as soon as the talking began, he began writing. Never absent for a single day, he kept a record of all that was said during the next four months, stopping only when he, himself, wanted to speak.

Shh! We're Writing the Constitution   51

They knew that there would be many arguments in this room, but they agreed that they didn't want the whole country listening in and taking sides. They would keep the proceedings a secret. So before every meeting the door was locked. Sentries[1] were stationed in the hall. And even though it turned out to be a hot summer, the windows were kept closed. Why should they risk eavesdroppers? Members were not supposed to write gossipy letters home. Nor to answer nosy questions. Nor to discuss their business with outsiders. Benjamin Franklin was the one who had to be watched. He meant no harm but he did love to talk, especially at parties, so if he seemed about to spill the beans, another delegate was ready to leap into the conversation and change the subject.

For fifty-five men to keep a secret for four months was an accomplishment in itself. But they did. Of course this didn't prevent rumors from starting. Once it was rumored that the convention was planning to invite the second son of George the Third to become King of America. The delegates were furious. They might not be able to say what they were going to do, but they had no trouble saying what they were *not* going to do. And they were not inviting the second or third son of George the Third or of anyone else to be King of America.

---

1. sentries: guards.

From *Shh! We're Writing the Constitution,* by Jean Fritz.

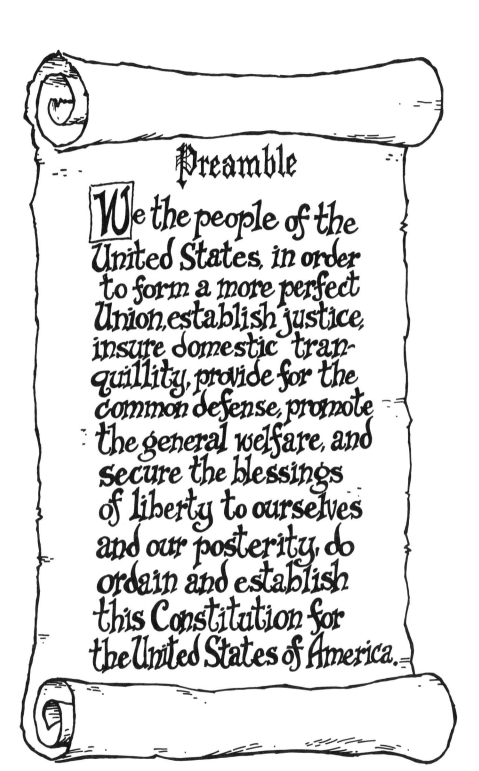

Preamble

We the people of the United States, in order to form a more perfect Union, establish justice, insure domestic tranquillity, provide for the common defense, promote the general welfare, and secure the blessings of liberty to ourselves and our posterity, do ordain and establish this Constitution for the United States of America.

Why are changes in official documents necessary? In 1791 ten amendments, known as the Bill of Rights, were added to the Constitution of the United States. Read these amendments to evaluate how they further protect your rights.

The Bill

Religious and political rights

Amendment I. Congress shall make no law respecting an establishment of religion, or prohibiting the free exercise thereof; or abridging the freedom of speech, or of the press; or the right of the people peaceably to assemble, and to petition the government for a redress of grievances.

Right to keep firearms

Amendment II. A well-regulated militia[1] being necessary to the security of a free state, the right of the people to keep and bear arms shall not be infringed.

Housing of soldiers

Amendment III. No soldier shall in time of peace be quartered in any house without the consent of the owner; nor in time of war, but in a manner to be prescribed by law.

Searches and seizures

Amendment IV. The right of the people to be secure in their persons, houses, papers, and effects, against unreasonable searches and seizures, shall not be violated; and no warrants shall issue but upon probable cause, supported by oath or affirmation, and particularly describing the place to be searched and the persons or things to be seized.

Rights of the accused

Amendment V. No person shall be held to answer for a capital[2] or otherwise infamous crime, unless on a presentment or indictment of a grand jury,[3] except in cases arising in the land or naval forces, or in the militia, when in actual service in time of war or public danger; nor shall any person be subject for the same offense to be twice put in jeopardy of life or limb, nor

---

1. militia: a citizen army called upon during emergencies.
2. capital crime: crime punishable by death.
3. grand jury: a group of 12 to 23 people that decides whether there is enough evidence against the accused to hold a trial.

# of Rights

shall be compelled in any criminal case to be a witness against himself, nor be deprived of life, liberty, or property, without due process[4] of law; nor shall private property be taken for public use without just compensation.

Right to a fair trial

Amendment VI. In all criminal prosecutions, the accused shall enjoy the right to a speedy and public trial, by an impartial jury of the state and district wherein the crime shall have been committed, which district shall have been previously ascertained by law, and to be informed of the nature and cause of the accusation; to be confronted with the witnesses against him; to have compulsory process for obtaining witnesses in his favor, and to have the assistance of counsel for his defense.

Rights in civil cases[5]

Amendment VII. In suits at common law, where the value in controversy shall exceed twenty dollars, the right of trial by jury shall be preserved, and no fact tried by a jury shall be otherwise re-examined in any court of the United States than according to the rules of the common law.

Bails, fines, and punishments

Amendment VIII. Excessive bail shall not be required, nor excessive fines imposed, nor cruel and unusual punishments inflicted.

Rights not listed

Amendment IX. The enumeration in the Constitution of certain rights shall not be construed to deny or disparage others retained by the people.

Powers of the states

Amendment X. The powers not delegated to the United States by the Constitution, nor prohibited by it to the states, are reserved to the states respectively or to the people.

---

4. due process: a set course for legal proceedings.
5. civil cases: money or property disputes.

What if you were denied rights guaranteed by the government? In 1837 Elijah P. Lovejoy died defending his rights to free speech and free press. Read the following selection to understand why Lovejoy fought so hard for his rights.

The Bill of Rights: Safeguard of Freedom

It seemed that everyone in town had squeezed into the meetinghouse. All eyes now turned to the front of the room where a pale young man faced the angry crowd, waiting for a chance to speak. He was there to demand protection from his enemies.

The speaker was Elijah P. Lovejoy, who in 1837 was the editor of a newspaper in Alton, Illinois. He had become highly unpopular because of his views on slavery. Most Americans of that day did not see anything wrong with owning slaves. But Lovejoy dared to tell his countrymen that blacks, no less than whites, had the right to be free. Because he insisted that all men are born free, the young editor was regarded as a troublemaker.

Some months before the town meeting, a gang of men and boys had broken into the building where Lovejoy's newspaper was printed and smashed the press. The leaders of the mob had thought that the young editor would be so frightened that he would leave town. But they underestimated their opponent. He set up another press and continued to print articles that demanded an end to slavery throughout the United States. When a mob destroyed the second printing press, Lovejoy got a third one.

It was after his third press had been destroyed by the mob that Lovejoy decided the time had come to remind the people of the town that even though his articles made them angry, he had the right to express his views. Not only that—he had the right to be protected from people who were breaking the laws of the United States by destroying his property.

The meetinghouse was a noisy place until the young editor began to speak. Then a great silence settled in the room:

> *I do not admit that it is the business of this assembly to decide whether I shall or shall not publish a newspaper in this city. . . . I have the right to do it. I know that I have the* RIGHT *freely to speak and publish my sentiments, subject only to the laws of the land for the abuse of that right. This right was given me by my Maker and is solemnly guaranteed to me by the Constitution of these United States and of this state.*

The audience did not like to hear what Lovejoy had to say about the rights given him by God and the Constitution. They liked it even less when he announced that he had ordered a fourth printing press and that he would continue to publish his newspaper.

Lovejoy had several friends at the meeting, and they were moved to tears by his speech. But the great majority of those present were angered by the editor's unwillingness to give up. His opponents took over the meeting, and made it clear that he would not be allowed to print his newspaper.

LOVEJOY'S RIGHTS ARE DEFENDED

Several leading citizens of the town were very disturbed when they realized that Lovejoy could expect no protection from the police. They knew that the mob would destroy the new press, as it had destroyed the earlier ones; that is, unless concerned citizens took matters into their own hands.

Not all the citizens who decided to defend Lovejoy agreed with his views on slavery. But they agreed that the Constitution gave him the right to print what he regarded as the truth.

Lovejoy's supporters armed themselves and made plans to deal with the mob.

Late one night, the new printing press was delivered to a stone warehouse that could be defended. News that Lovejoy had another press swept the town. A mob quickly gathered around the warehouse. The defenders opened the windows wide enough for rifles to show through. Members of the mob realized that the printing press was well defended.

Elijah P. Lovejoy.

The Bettmann Archive

Since they could not break down the walls of the warehouse, they decided to set fire to the roof.

Lovejoy saw several men placing a ladder against the wall. He ran outside the warehouse to knock the ladder down. A pistol shot rang out. The young editor fell to the ground.

The mob killed Lovejoy and destroyed his last printing press. But they did not destroy the ideas that he had laid before the people of the town. In fact, Lovejoy had more influence after he died than while he lived. The very fact that a young man had given up his life in defense of his beliefs caused many people to change their views on slavery. And as the report of Lovejoy's death was carried to all parts of the nation, the speech that he had made in defense of his rights was often quoted.

Through his death, Lovejoy reminded Americans that the government of their country is based on two important beliefs: (1) Human beings are born with certain rights that may not lawfully be taken from them, even by the government. (2) From these God-given rights, other rights develop as people live together and work out their differences. To protect citizens from the government that they set up, the rights of persons living in a democratic country are set down in the form of law. Usually these rights are outlined in the constitution, which is a statement that describes the organization of the government. In many cases, the rights of the people are set forth in a special part of the constitution. The Constitution of the United States contains such a section—the Bill of Rights. Elijah P. Lovejoy referred to that part of the Constitution in the last speech that he made.

Bill of Rights

Congress of the United States,

begun and held at the City of New York, on Wednesday, the fourth of March, one thousand seven hundred and eighty nine.

The Conventions of a number of the States having, at the time of their adopting the Constitution, expressed a desire, in order to prevent misconstruction or abuse of its powers, that further declaratory and restrictive clauses should be added: And as extending the ground of public confidence in the Government, will best insure the beneficent ends of its institution:

Resolved, by the SENATE and HOUSE of REPRESENTATIVES of the UNITED STATES of AMERICA in Congress assembled, two thirds of both Houses concurring. That the following Articles be proposed to the Legislatures of the several States, as Amendments to the Constitution of the United States; all, or any of which articles, when ratified by three fourths of the said Legislatures, to be valid to all intents and purposes, as part of the said Constitution, viz.

Articles in addition to, and Amendment of the Constitution of the United States of America, proposed by Congress, and ratified by the Legislatures of the several States, pursuant to the fifth Article of the Original Constitution.

Article the first ...... After the first enumeration required by the first Article of the Constitution, there shall be one Representative for every thirty thousand, until the number shall amount to one hundred, after which, the proportion shall be so regulated by Congress, that there shall be not less than one hundred Representatives, nor less than one Representative for every forty thousand persons, until the number of Representatives shall amount to two hundred, after which, the proportion shall be so regulated by Congress, that there shall not be less than two hundred Representatives, nor more than one Representative for every fifty thousand persons. [Not Ratified]

Article the second .... No law, varying the compensation for the services of the Senators and Representatives, shall take effect, until an election of Representatives shall have intervened. [Not Ratified]

Article the third .... Congress shall make no law respecting an establishment of religion, or prohibiting the free exercise thereof; or abridging the freedom of speech, or of the press; or the right of the people peaceably to assemble, and to petition the Government for a redress of grievances.

Article the fourth ..... A well regulated Militia, being necessary to the security of a free State, the right of the people to keep and bear Arms, shall not be infringed.

From *The Bill of Rights*, by E. B. Fincher.

How are laws made? The Constitution of the United States outlines a specific process to follow. Read this selection to learn more about the lawmaking process.

The Lawmaking Process

Powers to make laws are given to the Congress, which is made up of the Senate and the House of Representatives. The Senate and the House of Representatives are called "the houses of Congress." In these houses of Congress, no business can be transacted without a quorum. A quorum in each house is a majority of the members.

Laws, which are called bills before they are passed, may be started in either house of Congress. However, bills for revenue[1] must begin in the House of Representatives. After a bill is introduced, it is given a number and usually referred to a committee. There are 18 Senate Committees and 22 House Committees.

In a committee, detailed studies are made of the bill and hearings[2] may be held. A committee may amend, rewrite, recommend passage of, or ignore a bill. It is possible to pass some bills without committee approval, but this seldom happens.

Ten or fifteen thousand bills go into the hopper[3] during a session of Congress. Four out of five of these bills have little or no chance of being studied. Bills that seem unimportant to the committees are ignored. About one out of five bills is taken seriously, and public hearings on the bill may be held. After the committee finishes with this bill, it is reported to the house favorably or unfavorably. The whole house then votes on the bill.

The bills that come from committees are put on a calendar and voted on according to a schedule. Changes may be made and then the final vote is taken. The bill is sent to the next house of Congress if the vote is favorable.

In the second house of Congress the same type of procedure is followed. If the second house passes the bill, but in somewhat different form, a joint committee from both houses is set up to work out differences.

---

1. revenue: income that a government receives.
2. hearings: meetings to discuss pros and cons.
3. hopper: box for bills waiting to be considered.

How a Bill Becomes a Law

A bill can start in either house of Congress: the House of Representatives or the Senate. The diagram below shows a bill that starts in the House of Representatives. A bill passes through similar steps in the Senate.

1. A bill is introduced in the House of Representatives.

2. A committee studies the bill.

3. Public hearings may be held.

4. The committee reports its findings.

5. The House votes on the bill.

6. If a majority approves the bill, it goes to the Senate.

7. A committee studies the bill and reports its findings.

8. The Senate votes on the bill.

9. If a majority approves the bill, it goes to the President.

10. The President signs the bill and it becomes a law. Or the President vetoes the bill. A two-thirds vote in each house can still make it a law.

After the bill has passed the second house, it is sent to the President who has the choice of signing and approving the bill or vetoing (rejecting) the bill. If he signs it, it becomes another one of the laws of our land.

If the President does not sign the bill, but vetoes it, the two houses of Congress may try to pass it over the President's veto by a two-thirds vote in each house. However, very few bills pass this way.

If the President does not act at all, the bill becomes a law automatically in ten days, providing Congress is still in session. If Congress should adjourn before the ten-day period is up and the President does not act on the bill, it is automatically vetoed. This is called a pocket veto.

After Congress, the legislative branch, has passed a bill and the President, the executive branch, has signed the bill into law, it becomes the duty of the President to enforce it. The courts, the judicial branch, then interpret the law and administer justice under it, and the Supreme Court, the judicial branch, may rule whether or not the law is constitutional.

Lobbies

Our lawmakers in Congress feel the effect of pressure groups and lobbies. Pressure groups are groups of Americans interested in certain goals. Lobbies are the active parts of these pressure groups that seek to influence our legislators.[4] Some even provide helpful service to legislators by informing them how certain groups feel about important issues. However, a legislator must be careful that these lobbies do not exert too much influence and that views of other Americans are not overlooked. It is the right and the duty of organized groups to let their legislators know of their opinions on legislative matters, but we must be careful that these groups are kept within proper bounds. Therefore, lobbies are controlled by law.

---

4. legislators: lawmakers elected by the people.

From *Our Federal and State Constitutions*, by Alex J. Schmidt.

Unit 4: Behavioral Science

the study of why people act and feel the way they do

GOLCONDE, 1953, Rene Magritte, The Menil Collection, Houston.

How do you feel in a crowded elevator or when someone arrives late? Read the following selection for a better under-standing of people's attitudes toward time and personal space.

How People Use Space and Time

Space

Informal space refers to the space around us or the space we are occupying at the moment. The study of informal space is called *proxemics*. Managing your informal space requires some under-standing of attitudes toward space around us and attitudes toward our territory.

You are probably aware that communication is influenced by the distance between us and those with whom we communicate. Edward T. Hall, a leading researcher in nonverbal communication, has discussed the four different distances that most people perceive (*The Silent Language* [Garden City, N.Y.: Doubleday, 1959], 163-164). By far the most important to us is the intimate[1] distance, up to about eighteen inches from us, which we regard as appropriate for intimate conversation with close friends, parents, and younger children. People usually become uncomfortable when "outsiders" violate this intimate distance. Consider your last ride in a crowded elevator, for example. Most people get rather rigid, look at the floor

---

1. **intimate**: very close, deeply personal.

or the indicator above the door, and pretend that they are not touching. Being forced into an intimate situation is only acceptable when all involved follow the "rules." When there is no apparent good reason for your intimate space to be intruded upon, you may be alarmed. Notice people coming into a movie theater that is less than one-quarter full: Couples tend to leave a seat or more between them and another couple. If you are sitting in a nearly empty theater and a stranger sits right next to you, you are likely to be upset; if a person you do not know violates this intimate distance in conversation, you may move away instinctively.

The other three distances are personal—eighteen inches to four feet—appropriate for casual conversation; social—four to twelve feet—for impersonal business (a job interview, for instance); and public distance—more than twelve feet. Determining these four distances was not some arbitrary[2] decision; these are descriptions of what most people consider appropriate in various situations. Individuals do, of course, vary. Oftentimes problems occur when one person has for one reason or another developed a slightly different standard. For instance, Paul may come from a family that conducts informal conversations with others at a range closer than the eighteen-inch limit that most Americans place on intimate space. So, when Paul talks to Dan or Mary, people he has met in class for the first time, he may move in closer than eighteen inches for his conversation. He then may be very much surprised when both Dan and Mary seem to be backing away from him during the conversation.

Normally our intimate or personal space moves when we move, for we are likely to define these spaces as distances from us. Yet in many situations we seek to put claim to a given space around us whether we are occupying it currently or not—that is, we are likely to look at certain space as our *territory*. Territory is space over which a person claims ownership. If Marcia decides to eat lunch at the school cafeteria, the space at the table she selects becomes her territory. Let's say that Marcia goes back to the food area to get butter for her roll. The chair she left, the food on the table, and the space around that food are "hers" and she will expect others to stay away. If while she is eating her lunch someone across the table moves a glass or a dish into the area that Marcia sees as her territory, she may be at least a little upset.

2. arbitrary: unfounded or impulsive.

Many people stake out their territory with markers. George is planning to eat in the cafeteria. Before he gets his food he finds an empty table and puts his books on the table and his coat on a chair. These objects are indicators of occupied territory. If someone came along while George was gone and put the books and coat on the floor and then occupied that space, that person would be in big trouble when George returned.

Our needs for territory and the way we treat territory are culturally determined. As a result, what an American would consider the boundaries of territory may be different from what an Arab or an Asian would consider to be territorial boundaries. Misunderstandings between people of different cultures often occur as a result of their different ways of perceiving territory.

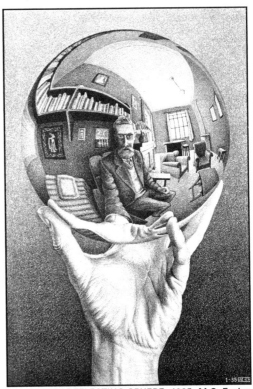

HAND WITH REFLECTING SPHERE, 1935, M.C. Escher, 1898-1972, National Gallery of Art, Washington, D.C., Rosenwald Collection.

Thus in our management of personal space we must understand that others may not look at either the space around us or our territory in quite the same way as we do. Because the majority of Americans have learned the same basic rules does not mean that everyone has or will treat either the respect for the rules or the consequences of breaking the rules in the same way.

Time

Although we have no control over time, how we manage our time and how we react to others' use and management of time are important aspects of personal style.

For each of us there is a length of time that we regard as appropriate for certain events. For instance, Sunday sermons are 20 to 30 minutes, classes are 50 minutes (Tuesday and Thursday classes of

75 minutes never seem right to many of us), a movie is roughly two hours. Television programs are 30 minutes or 60 minutes *unless* they are movies or sporting events. When the length of an event does not meet our expectation, that time itself becomes an obstacle to communication. We get angry with the professor who holds us beyond normal class time; we become hostile if someone asks us to cut short our lunch hour or coffee break.

In addition to an appropriate length of time there is also an appropriate time of day for certain things to happen. We work during the day, sleep at night, eat at noon, and so on. We make judgments about people who accept a "time" for events that differs from ours. Joe is strange if he gets up at 4:30 a.m. The Martins eat dinner at 4:30 p.m. and the Smiths don't dine till 8 p.m.—we may consider both families peculiar. Adam works on his books from midnight until 4 a.m. and then sleeps till noon—we are aware that he is "different." So, *when* people do things communicates something to us.

But perhaps most basic to our perception of people is how they treat time designations. For instance, suppose you are holding a party. When you invited people you told them to come at about 8 p.m. What do you think of Rob (a) if he arrives at 7:30? (b) if he arrives at 8 p.m. exactly? (c) if he arrives at 8:30? (d) if he arrives at 10 p.m.? Now, for sake of argument, let's change the setting. Suppose you have a test scheduled for tomorrow. After today's class, suppose that a group of five of you decides to study together. Since your place is as good as any you say, "Stop by about 8 p.m." Now what do you think of Rob (a) he arrives at 7:30? (b) 8 p.m. exactly? (c) 8:30? and (d) 10 p.m.? Depending upon how you see time, you will make a value judgment upon the basis of when he comes; moreover, you may view his arrival time differently depending upon the occasion.

Time does communicate. We must be sensitive to our own perceptions of time, as well as those of others, so that the variable of time facilitates or at least does not inhibit[3] communication.

---

3. **inhibit:** hold back.

From *Communicate! 3/E*, by Rudolph F. Verderber.

How do you learn best? The following selection contains 25 true or false statements. By answering the statements and reading the explanations that follow, you may gain insight into your best learning style.

What's Your Learning Style?

For Donna Lance, homework is usually 20 minutes of serious studying interspersed with forays to the kitchen or game room. Lance is a reader, and only when she looks over her notes and books does the lecture she heard in class finally sink in.

Nothing ruins Sandy Donovan's concentration more than a break. Donovan is a listener. He studies with a friend, reading notes aloud and thinking of questions that might be asked in class. Or he retreats to the language lab, where the French that seems so alien in print comes alive through the headphones.

Research has shown that everyone has a unique learning style. You may need prodding and encouragement, or you may buckle down on your own. You may study best in the morning, or you may be a better afternoon learner. All this has little to do with moods, but a lot to do with inborn preferences.

This quiz will identify some aspects of your learning style. And it will alert you to your natural strengths—which you can use to overcome learning difficulty.

If the questions sound basic, there's a reason—they were selected from the Learning Style Inventory, a lengthy computer-scored quiz that has been simplified but is still accurate. Answer each question in the box "True" or "False." Your first, spontaneous response is probably the truest answer you can give. Here goes.

1. I really like to listen to people talk.

2. I really like to watch television.

3. I must be reminded often to do something.

4. I can sit in one place for a long time.

5. If I could go to school anytime during the day, I'd go in the morning.

6. I really like people to talk to me.

7. The things I remember best are those I see.

8. I don't have to be reminded to do something.

9. I can't sit in one place for a long time.

10. If I could go to school at any time during the day, I'd go in the early evening.

11. I'd rather read than listen to a lecture.

12. I prefer to learn something new by having it told to me.

13. I forget to do things I've been told to do.

14. I find it hard to sit in one place for a long time.

15. I remember things best when I study them in the early morning.

16. I find it easy to listen to people talk.

17. It's easy for me to remember what I see.

18. I remember what I'm told to do.

19. I have to get up and move around when I study.

20. I remember things best when I study them in the evening.

21. I enjoy learning by listening.

22. I like to learn by reading.

23. I do what I'm expected to do.

24. It's easy for me to stay put when I study.

25. I study best in the morning.

each area, a score of 3 means that you're adaptable and that you possibly lean toward a higher score.)

Do you learn best by seeing?

If you answered "True" to four or five of questions 2, 7, 11, 17, and 22, you absorb new material better by reading it (unless you scored high as a listener, too, and have both strengths). Students who find it difficult to learn by hearing should ask their teachers for printed handouts or more examples on the board—something they can relate to visually. Price says teachers are often more receptive to such requests than students expect.

If you're in a lecture class, take notes, ask to have things diagrammed, and seek out films, books, or articles on things you didn't quite grasp in class.

If you answered "True" to two or fewer questions in this area and also

Do you learn best by hearing?

Answering "True" to four or five of questions 1, 6, 12, 16, and 21, says Dr. Gary Price, author of the original Learning Style Inventory, indicates that you'd rather learn by hearing. "You like to be told things," notes Price. Reading the same material in silence, on the other hand, may leave you cold. If you score high as a listener, Price advises that you study with someone else and stop occasionally to talk over the information. Some students report that when they study alone or read test questions in class, they do better if they imagine *hearing* the words. Listen to your "mind's ear" when you read.

If you answered "True" to two or fewer questions, you may be better off *seeing* what you want to learn. (As in

ENTER TIME AND DATE NOW.

DON'T FORGET TO SAVE!

scored low as a listener, you probably prefer what teachers call multisensory instruction. Seeing, hearing, *and* touching may work best for you. Such hands-on learning often includes working with computers, watching films, or taking language labs that use both recorded and visual materials.

"There is no good or bad learning style," Price stresses. "The sooner you know how you prefer to learn, the easier learning is."

Do you work well on your own?

Score a point for each "True" answer to questions 8, 18, and 23; score a point for each "False" answer to questions 3 and 13.

How efficiently you handle work assignments often indicates how well you work on your own—and how responsible you are. Most students score high on responsibility, but their teachers may see them as irresponsible. This is often because a student is hostile[1] toward authority figures, says Price, not because he's lazy.

If you scored four or five points, you can handle a research project or paper on your own. You tend to be a high achiever, at least in areas that interest you. You don't need a lot of feedback[2] while you're working, but you definitely seek recognition when you're done.

If you scored two or fewer points, you may need more feedback while you work. You work best on short assignments—even if you must do more of them. It helps if you get reactions to your progress along the way. Long texts may be less motivating and rewarding for you than workbooks that break material down into bite-sized segments followed by short quizzes.

If you scored low in this area, examine your feelings about being told what to do, and try to separate them from the learning challenge that confronts you.

Are you a mover or a sitter?

Score a point for each "True" answer to questions 9, 14, and 19 and a point for each "False" answer to questions 4 and 24.

If you scored 4 or 5, you're probably miserable sitting in the library or at your desk for a long time. You need breaks—if only to stretch—every half hour or so. Listen to your body and take them.

If you're a mover and confined to your desk, try this breathing exercise:

---

1. **hostile:** very unfriendly.
2. **feedback:** information on effectiveness.

Inhale deeply and imagine the air flowing down through your chest, stomach, thighs, and legs—right to your toes. Then exhale, drawing the air back up through your toes, legs, torso, and out of your mouth. Relax your jaw, since that's where tension tends to build. A few deep breaths may satisfy the urge to wander.

The need to move around, Price says, often goes with the desire to eat while working. Both are distractions, but to many students they're important ones. Some teachers become distressed when students munch in class, but, says Price, more liberal teachers have started providing carrot and celery sticks to students who want them.

If you scored two or fewer points, moving around is a useless distraction for you. Sitting still, often in an uncluttered environment, allows you to absorb material without losing your train of thought. Study when and where the only interruptions are those you choose.

When do you learn best?
Score a point for each "True" answer to questions 5, 15, and 25 and one for each "False" answer to questions 10 and 20.

If you scored 4 or 5, you're probably a morning learner. Take your most challenging classes early, and don't start your homework on Sunday night. If you scored low, you reach your peak in the late morning or afternoon and should plan your most challenging work accordingly.

Afternoon learners aren't lazy; they're simply in touch with a biological preference that school often doesn't accommodate. Similarly, morning learners may wind down by midafternoon. One research study found that students were less likely to be late to or cut classes that were scheduled at a preferred time.

"Teachers should find out how their students learn and be sensitive to individual differences," Price notes. Ultimately, though, learning is up to you. And knowing how you learn best can help you learn better.

"What's Your Learning Style?" by Dylan Landis. Reprinted with permission from *Sourcebook*. Copyright 1982, Whittle Communications L.P.

Do you eat three well-balanced meals each day? When time is short, many people grab a snack instead of eating a well-balanced meal. Read the following selection to learn more about snacks that are quick and healthy, too.

The "Grazing" of America:
A Guide to Healthy Snacking

Sheep do it. Horses do it. Cows do it. Now even children, teenagers, and seniors are doing it.

"Grazing" is fast becoming the American way of eating, according to nutritionists. "Since everyone is always rushing around in a hurry these days, there's often no time for three square meals. So grazing, or snacking on mini-meals, becomes important," says Marilyn Stephenson, a registered dietician and assistant to the director, office of nutrition and food science, Food and Drug Administration.

Grazing is a way of filling in those necessary calories and nutrients you might otherwise miss due to incomplete or skipped meals. Done wisely, grazing is not only good for you, it can be fun, too. Grazing isn't just milk and cookies. It's finding creative, but nonfattening, ways to enrich your diet with protein, complex carbohydrates, vitamins, and minerals.

How you graze and what you choose to graze on should depend on your age and lifestyle. For instance, adults must be more careful than children about snacking. Because the amount of energy needed to fuel basic body functions decreases as one gets older, it takes fewer calories to maintain the body. Also, adults tend to become less physically active over the years, which further decreases their calorie needs. So long as total calories are kept in mind, though, there's nothing wrong with grazing if snacks are well planned to include essential nutrients.

Calorie Salary

Jennifer Anderson, a registered dietician and assistant professor in the department of food science and human nutrition at Colorado State University, says snacking is easy for adults if they obey the "calorie-salary rule." Determine your daily "salary" of calories, and make sure you "spend" no more than that over the course of your meals and snacks for the day.

For example, if you know you'll be eating lots of food at a party, eat low-calorie foods the rest of the day. Or, if you eat a large lunch, balance out the extra calories you consumed with a low-calorie supper, such as a salad. If you do find yourself eating more calories than usual in a day, increase your physical activity, says Anderson. Exercise helps to burn up those extra calories.

And beware of pseudo[1]-nutritious "health" foods. When craving sweets, if you're thinking of choosing a granola bar instead of a conventional candy bar because you think it is more healthful, don't. Registered dietician Gail Levey, spokeswoman for the American Dietetic Association, warns that "Granola bars are just packed with grease. A granola bar

sounds so wholesome, but to get it to stick together you have to use so much fat." On average, about 35 percent of the calories in many of the granola bars comes from fat, whereas approximately 46 percent of calories in candy bars is from fat.

The *Dietary Guidelines for Americans* from the Departments of Agriculture and Health and Human Services advises Americans to avoid too much fat and cholesterol[2] in their diets. Fat, especially saturated fat,[3] raises the level of cholesterol in the blood, which is, in turn, a risk factor for heart disease. There is also evidence that a high dietary fat intake may be associated with certain types of cancer. Both the American Heart Association and the National Cancer Institute recommend that Americans reduce their fat intake to about 30 percent of their total calories.

More Fat, More Calories

Less than one-third of the fat in the diet should be in the form of saturated fats, such as butter and lard. The remainder should be from monounsaturated or polyunsaturated sources, which help decrease blood cholesterol levels.

Fats are a dense source of calories. Both protein and carbohydrates have four calories per gram; fats have nine. So any time you have a fat-filled

---

1. **pseudo:** false.
2. **cholesterol:** a fat-like substance in blood, tissues, and food.
3. **saturated fat:** fat that usually is solid at room temperature. It contains molecules that do not unite easily with other compounds.

snack, it's likely to be relatively high in calories.

Some foods people choose for small snacks contain 10 or more grams of fat. "That's quite a bit for one serving of a snack food," according to Bonnie Liebman, director of nutrition, Center for Science in the Public Interest, a Washington, D.C.-based consumer advocacy group. "I advise people looking for low-fat frozen dinners to choose products that contain less than 10 grams—and that's for a full meal or an entree."

Reducing one's fat intake doesn't have to mean a life of austere[4] eating, but it does require making sensible choices and substitutions. Choose dairy products low in fat. Ice milk, for example, has less than half the fat of ice cream and approximately 40 percent fewer calories. Tofutti, a frozen dessert made from tofu (a soybean-based food), contains no cholesterol, but has almost twice the fat of ordinary ice cream. And although plain and flavored frozen yogurts have less fat than ice cream, they don't offer many calorie savings.

Seventy-five percent of the calories in most hard cheeses comes from fat. Your best option is to snack on cheeses made primarily from skim milk, such as pot cheese, part-skim ricotta, cottage cheese, skim farmer cheeses, and many diet cheeses and other low-fat cheeses.

Spread the cheese on whole-grain crackers or bread, or eat it with an apple or celery for a snack low in fat, but high in fiber.

Also, choose plain, low-fat yogurt as a snack instead of yogurt with fruit, which is sweetened and contains more calories. Not only will you save on calories, but you'll be able to add your own low-calorie fresh fruit and dry toppings, such as wheat germ, to make it a more nutritious snack.

Snack sparingly on nuts. Nuts are high in fat and, therefore, high in calories, as well. Instead, choose, for example, freshly popped corn, air-popped, rather than popped in oil. But remember that adding butter to it will add fat and calories.

Popular snack foods, such as chips, pretzels, and packaged popcorn, may contain large amounts of salt. "Pretzels and some brands of popcorn, for example, often contain up to 950 milligrams of sodium per serving—quite a bit when adults should get no more than 1,100 to 3,300 milligrams a day," according to Liebman.

Eating too much sodium (salt is sodium chloride) is associated with high blood pressure—a major risk factor for heart attack, stroke, and kidney disease in some people.

Older adults especially should watch their sodium intake because of the prevalence[5] of high blood pressure and heart disease in their age group.

---

4. austere: strict, pleasureless.
5. prevalence: common occurrence.

Elder Grazers

Older adults often rely on grazing for most of their calories, so it's important that they keep a variety of nutritious snack foods on hand. A good snack for this age group, according to Barbara Deskins, a registered dietician and associate professor at the University of Pittsburgh, is one that supplies calcium, as well as other nutrients, because many older adults don't get enough calcium in their diets.

She suggests a glass of low-fat milk, cubes of low-fat cheese, or low-fat yogurt for a snack high in calcium, protein, some B vitamins, vitamin A, and, if fortified, vitamin D. Tuna fish sandwiches or roast chicken with the skin removed are also nutritious snacks, providing protein, iron, B vitamins, and zinc. Whole-grain oatmeal cookies, graham crackers, and raw vegetables are good sources of dietary fiber and may provide some vitamin A, vitamin C, B vitamins, and iron.

Anderson of Colorado State says that choosing snacks lower in fat, sugar, and sodium is easier for everyone if the right snacks are kept on hand. She suggests stocking the refrigerator with a variety of healthful leftovers, keeping a supply of "transportable" snacks, such as small cans of juice, fresh fruits and vegetables, crackers, and cheese cubes. Quick and easy fixings like yogurt and fruit should also be on hand for puréeing in a blender to make nutritious instant shakes.

Toddlers Need to Snack

What children need by way of a nutritious snack differs from what is recommended for older adults. Foods

children graze on will often set the stage for what they'll choose as snacks later in life. Children under 2 require a lot of calories to fuel their rapid growth. However, their appetites and stomachs are so small that they often can't eat enough at their regular meals to meet their daily demands. So they *need* to graze. Many nutritionists recommend several little meals in place of three big ones for this age group. (Parents need to watch their toddlers carefully during snack times to guard against choking.)

Lightly cooked vegetables, such as broccoli and green beans, and tender, bite-size pieces of meat, poultry, and fruit are good finger foods for this age group. So are dry breakfast cereals, tiny sandwiches, and crackers. Small amounts of spaghetti and pizza also make good snacks.

Milk, yogurt, and small cubes of cheese make wonderful snacks, too, because the calcium they supply helps in teeth and bone formation.

A statement by the American Heart Association, the American Health Foundation, and a consensus development panel sponsored by the National Institutes of Health recommended in

1986 that Americans reduce their fat and cholesterol intakes to help decrease the risk of coronary heart disease. But the statement excluded children under 2 from this recommendation. Nevertheless, many well-meaning parents have adopted a low-fat, restricted-calorie diet for their children as well as themselves. As a result, there have been medical reports of decreased growth rate and poor weight gain among some toddlers.

Overzealous Parents

Concerned that parents' zeal[6] for low-fat diets would adversely[7] affect their children's growth and health, the American Academy of Pediatrics issued a statement in 1986 that for children, "the current dietary trends in the United States—decreased consumption of saturated fats, cholesterol, and salt and an increased intake of polyunsaturated fats—should be followed with moderation. The optimal fat intake cannot be determined, but 30 percent to 40 percent of total calories seems sensible for adequate growth and development. Diets that avoid extremes are safe for children for whom there is no evidence of special vulnerability."[8]

The academy also found no "compelling new evidence to make recommendations concerning modification of the diet" for teenagers, either.

Like young children, teenagers are constantly growing, and many need frequent extra helpings of foods to provide them with enough protein, vitamins, minerals, and calories to meet their growth and energy needs. Teenagers who participate in sports need even more calories to maintain their body weight.

No single food supplies all of the essential nutrients in the amounts the body needs, so it is important, especially for growing children, to eat a variety of foods. Eating foods from each of the following four food groups daily helps to ensure a balanced diet:

- fruits and vegetables;
- meat, poultry, fish, eggs, and dried beans and peas;
- milk and cheese; and
- whole-grain breads and cereals.

Bread, cereals, and other grain products provide B vitamins, iron, protein, and fiber. Fruits and vegetables are good sources of vitamin A, vitamin C, folic acid, fiber, and many minerals. Meats, poultry, fish, eggs, and dried beans and peas supply protein, iron and other minerals, as well as several B vitamins. Milk and cheese are major sources of calcium—very important in the diets of children and teenagers. Storing as much calcium as possible in the bones in younger years may help prevent osteoporosis later in life. Osteoporosis, brought on by loss of bone mass, causes bones to fracture more easily.

---

6. zeal: eagerness or enthusiasm.
7. adversely: unfavorably, harmfully.
8. vulnerability: weakness.

Teen Snacks

Though teenagers can benefit from snacking, they often fall into the habit of constantly eating the same foods. Snacks sometimes even substitute for, rather than supplement, regular meals. And snack foods may not provide the variety of nutrients these youngsters need. For example, a soda that replaces milk at lunch may reduce the amount of calcium in the diet.

Teenagers who like to snack on soft drinks should be encouraged to have a cheeseburger, rather than a plain burger, with their drink. A slice of cheese pizza is another good snack that will add calcium to the diet.

Snacks high in fiber are also a good choice for teenagers because they stimulate salivation, which helps wash away excess sugar accumulated naturally or from such sugary snacks as candy bars. This reduces the chance of tooth decay, according to the Academy of General Dentistry.

High-fiber snacks include popcorn, fruits and vegetables (especially with skins and seeds), dried peas and beans, nuts, and whole-grain foods and other whole-grain cereal products. In addition to dietary fiber, these foods provide vitamins and minerals that are essential for normal growth, development, and metabolism.[9]

While snacking is regarded as a potential asset to the teenager's diet, it can become a liability if it results in more calories than are needed. Obesity often starts during the teenage years.

---

9. metabolism: the process by which the body uses food for energy.

For the Calorie-Conscious Snacker

Almost No Calories Per Serving
Celery sticks
Lettuce
Cucumbers
Green peppers
Mushrooms
Cauliflower
Broccoli

25-30 Calories
1 small tangerine
1/2 cup watermelon
1/4 cantaloupe
1 small tomato
1 medium carrot
1 cup popcorn
12 pretzel sticks

35-40 Calories
1 medium peach
1 medium nectarine
1/2 grapefruit
1/2 cup skim milk
1/4 cup plain yogurt
3 saltine crackers
1/2 small banana

50-60 Calories
1 small apple
1 small orange
15 grapes
12 cherries
1 cup strawberries
1/4 cup cottage cheese
4 small shrimp

From "The 'Grazing' of America," by Cheryl Platzman Weinstock, *FDA Consumer,* March 1989.

What makes you happy? Read the following selection to consider one person's ideas about the nature of happiness.

MAN GLOWING WITH HAPPINESS, 1968, Ruffino Tamayo, Museo Ruffino Tamayo, Mexico City. Photograph by Jesus Sanchez Uribe.

The Secret of True Happiness

I live in the land of Disney, Hollywood, and year-round sun. You may think people in such a glamorous, fun-filled place are happier than others. If so, you have some mistaken ideas about the nature of happiness.

Many intelligent people still equate happiness with fun. The truth is that fun and happiness have little or nothing in common. Fun is what we experience *during* an act. Happiness is what we experience *after* an act. It is a deeper, more abiding[1] emotion.

Going to an amusement park or ball game, watching a movie or television, are fun activities that help us relax, temporarily forget our problems, and maybe even laugh. But they do not bring happiness, because their positive effects end when the fun ends.

I have often thought that if Hollywood stars have a role to play, it is to teach us that happiness has nothing to do with fun. These rich, beautiful individuals have constant access to glamorous parties, fancy cars, expensive homes—everything that spells "happiness." But in memoir after memoir, celebrities reveal the unhappiness hidden beneath all their fun: depression, alcoholism, drug addiction, broken marriages, troubled children, profound loneliness.

Yet people continue to believe that the next, more glamorous party, more expensive car, more luxurious vacation, fancier home will do what all the other parties, cars, vacations, homes have not been able to do.

The way people cling to the belief that a fun-filled, pain-free life equals happiness actually diminishes[2]

---

1. abiding: lasting.
2. diminishes: reduces.

their chances of ever attaining real happiness. If fun and pleasure are equated with happiness, then pain must be equated with unhappiness. But, in fact, the opposite is true: *More times than not, things that lead to happiness involve some pain.*

As a result, many people avoid the very endeavors[3] that are the source of true happiness. They fear the pain inevitably[4] brought by such things as marriage, raising children, professional achievement, religious commitment, civic or charitable work, self-improvement.

Ask a bachelor why he resists marriage even though he finds dating to be less and less satisfying. If he's honest, he will tell you that he is afraid of making a commitment. For commitment is in fact quite painful. The single life is filled with fun, adventure, excitement. Marriage has such moments, but they are not its most distinguishing features.

Similarly, couples who choose not to have children are deciding in favor of painless fun over painful happiness. They can dine out whenever they want, travel wherever they want, and sleep as late as they want. Couples with infant children are lucky to get a whole night's sleep or a three-day vacation. I don't know any parent who would choose the word *fun* to describe raising children.

But couples who decide not to have children never experience the pleasure of hugging them or tucking them into bed at night. They never know the joys of watching a child grow up or of playing with a grandchild.

Of course I enjoy doing fun things. I like to play racquetball, joke with kids (and anybody else), and I probably have too many hobbies.

But these forms of fun do not contribute in any real way to my happiness. More difficult endeavors—writing, raising children, creating a deep relationship with my wife, trying to do good in the world—will bring me more happiness than can ever be found in fun, that least permanent of things.

Understanding and accepting that true happiness has nothing to do with fun is one of the most liberating[5] realizations we can ever come to. It liberates time: now we can devote more hours to activities that can genuinely increase our happiness. It liberates money: buying that new car or those fancy clothes that will do nothing to increase our happiness now seems pointless. And it liberates us from envy: we now understand that all those rich and glamorous people we were so sure are happy because they are always having so much fun actually may not be happy at all.

The moment we understand that fun does not bring happiness, we begin to lead our lives differently. The effect can be, quite literally, life-transforming.

---

3. **endeavors**: efforts.
4. **inevitably**: certainly.
5. **liberating**: freeing.

From "The Secret of True Happiness," by Dennis Prager. Dennis Prager writes and publishes a quarterly journal about life, *Ultimate Issues*, 6020 Washington Blvd., Culver City, California 90232.

Unit 5: Economics

the study of how goods and services are produced, distributed, and consumed

DOLLAR SIGNS, 1981, Andy Warhol, copyright 1990, The Estate and Foundation of Andy Warhol / ARS N.Y.

Do you wish your money would stretch further? Read the following selection for tips on setting goals and budgeting that may help you make the most of your money.

Making Ends Meet

Do you find it harder and harder to make ends meet? If you do, you're not alone. It's increasingly important, therefore, to budget. Budgeting—setting goals and tracking your progress toward them—helps to make the most of your income, whatever that income is.

Identify Your Goals And Objectives

Before you can draw up a budget, you have to know what you're budgeting *for*. You have to identify both your goals (your financial destination) and your objectives (the step-by-step path toward the goal). If your goal is to buy a house, for example, your objectives might include building enough cash reserves for a down payment and ensuring sufficient income to manage the carrying costs.

Don't assume that goals and objectives are obvious. If you are married, you may find after talking it over that you and your spouse have somewhat different priorities. One of you may feel that owning a home should be the primary goal while the other may believe that it's more important, if a choice must be made, to provide a college education for the children. You won't know unless you discuss your goals and assess their importance. If you are single, you may learn some interesting things about your own goals by thinking them through and ranking them in order of importance.

Drawing Up A Budget

Despite their reputation as a tedious bore, budgets are a very useful tool for managing your money. A budget measures what you have against what you spend. With a budget, you can bring income and outgo in line, stop spending in nonproductive and unsatisfying ways, and trim excess spending so that you can save for the future. But a budget can do these things only if it's a budget you can live with. There's no point in drawing up elaborate budget charts and then dropping the whole idea because it's just too complicated. Here are some workable techniques:

1. Seeing where your money goes

This basic budgeting technique reviews the past rather than forecasting the future. It involves keeping track, for a limited period of time, of every penny you spend. Carry a pocket notebook and record every newspaper, bus fare, haircut, and cup of coffee, as well as every bag of groceries, pair of shoes, and appliance repair. Do this for a month or two and you'll have a clear picture of where your money actually goes. Then, without continuing the record-keeping, you'll be able to cut back on little expenditures that add up without giving you much pleasure.

2. Setting money aside

This goal-oriented budget can be useful if you have one overriding goal and if you're not living too close to the margin[1] to begin with. If you know, for example, that you will need $2,000 to paint your house a year from now, divide that $2,000 by 12 and force yourself to save $166 every month. (You'll actually need to

---

1. margin: bare minimum.

save less, because your savings will be earning interest as they grow.) If you know that you must paint the house, you'll take the $166 off the top of your take-home pay each month without fail. Pretend you took a cut in salary, and arrange the rest of your spending accordingly.

This budget can help you reach a specific goal, but it isn't perfect by any means. It's essentially a limited venture, not the kind of tool that will help you control all your financial affairs.

3. Using envelopes, jars, and piggy banks

This familiar method, in which you allocate[2] all your take-home pay by category (rent, food, clothing, and so on), is all-inclusive and therefore a more useful version of the set-aside budget. It's an operating tool, rather than a planning tool, but it will help you gain control of your spending. Just be careful; if you find yourself constantly borrowing from one envelope to fund another, your system needs review.

4. Identifying income and outgo

The most useful method of budgeting, however, is the most detailed. It involves identifying all your current income and outgo, then projecting income and outgo into the future. It takes some time to set up this type of budget, but keeping it up to date, if you do so regularly, will be easy.

Here's what to do: On a single sheet of paper, list all your definite sources of income for this year—salary, interest, dividends, commissions, rent, and so on. Use after-tax, take-home income to work with, because it's only spendable income that you should allocate. Then, in parallel columns, list your projected income a year from now. Don't count on an anticipated tax refund until it is in hand. Count only income you're sure of; overtime and bonuses, even if they've been standard in your company for years, are not guaranteed.

Once income is defined, look at outgo, both now and a year from now. List outgo in terms of categories, from fixed (housing, insurance, taxes) to variable[3] (food, housing repair and maintenance,

---

2. allocate: divide.
3. variable: changeable.

clothing, medical care, transportation, charitable contributions). At the bottom, include optional items (entertainment, recreation, travel, gifts, hobbies). List all your outgo on a monthly basis, so that you can allocate funds ahead of time for an annual insurance premium or a semiannual tuition bill. To make the task easier, round all figures to the nearest five dollars.

A budget is a form of financial self-portrait. But whether you choose a rough sketch or a detailed portrait for your budget, it will work best for you if you:

• Review it regularly to be sure it's up to date and serving your needs. Your needs change as your life changes and a budget, to be useful, must change as well.

• Include adequate provision for taxes, especially if you will owe tax over and above what is withheld from salary.

• Include an inflation factor in your budget, using the inflation rate for the preceding year to determine how much more money you'll need.

• Shop wisely to build your savings and reach long-term goals.

From *Making Ends Meet,* by Grace W. Weinstein.

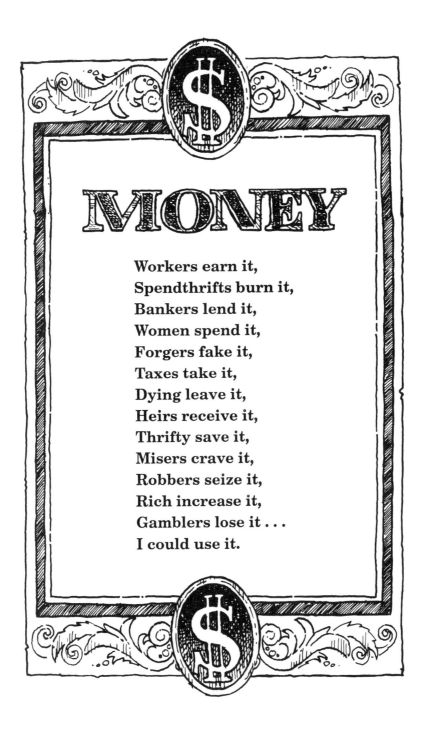

MONEY

Workers earn it,
Spendthrifts burn it,
Bankers lend it,
Women spend it,
Forgers fake it,
Taxes take it,
Dying leave it,
Heirs receive it,
Thrifty save it,
Misers crave it,
Robbers seize it,
Rich increase it,
Gamblers lose it . . .
I could use it.

"Money" by Richard Armour. Permission by Branden Publishing Company, Boston.

What do you do if you are dissatisfied with a product or service? Read the following selection to find out how to handle product or service complaints.

NEW SHOES FOR H, 1973, Don Eddy, The Cleveland Museum of Art, Purchased with a grant from the National Endowment for the Arts and matched with a gift from members of the Cleveland Society for Contemporary Art, CMA 74.53.

Consumerism

Consumerism is a movement that promotes the interests of buyers of goods and services. It works to protect consumers from unsafe or low-quality products; fraudulent[1] advertising, labeling, or packaging; and business practices that limit competition. Consumerism, also known as *consumer protection* or the *consumer movement,* is active in many countries. This article discusses the movement in the United States.

Consumerism includes activities by consumers themselves, as well as government action on the federal, state, and local level. The movement seeks to provide adequate information about products so that consumers can make wise decisions in purchasing goods and services. Consumerism also tries to inform consumers of effective means of obtaining compensation[2] for damage or injury caused by defective products.

The rise of the consumer movement has had major effects on business and industry. Many companies have become more responsive to the needs, wants, and safety of consumers. Other firms have not been responsive to these concerns. Some of them have experienced financial losses and unfavorable publicity resulting

---

1. fraudulent: dishonest.
2. compensation: suitable payment.

from lawsuits by dissatisfied consumers and government-ordered recalls of defective products.

The Consumer's Rights

Consumer groups and many other people believe consumers have several basic rights. For example, they believe consumers are entitled to (1) products whose quality is consistent with their prices and the claims of manufacturers; (2) protection against unsafe goods; (3) truthful, adequate information about goods or services; and (4) a choice among a variety of products. Buyers also have certain responsibilities. For example, they must use a product for the purpose intended by the manufacturer, and they should follow the instructions provided with the product.

The right to quality. Warranties and money-back guarantees provide assurances that a product will live up to the claims of the manufacturer. Most warranties are written statements that promise repair, replacement, or a refund if a product fails to perform as the manufacturer said it would for a certain period of time. A money-back guarantee promises a refund of the purchase price if the buyer is not completely satisfied.

The Magnuson-Moss Warranty Act of 1975 helps regulate warranties. This law requires that warranties be written clearly so they can be easily understood by the public. The act also gives the consumer the right to an *implied warranty* if the manufacturer does not provide a written warranty. An implied warranty is an unwritten guarantee that a product is suitable for the purpose for which it has been sold. For example, a hair drier should dry hair. Only a product sold "as is" has no implied warranty. Such goods include damaged and second-hand items.

The right to safety. A number of agencies of the federal government play an important role in ensuring the safety of goods. For example, the Food and Drug Administration (FDA) enforces laws concerning the safety of food, drugs, and cosmetics. The Consumer Product Safety Commission sets safety standards for many household products. The National Highway Traffic Safety Administration sets and enforces safety requirements for automobiles and related products. All such agencies test products and inspect factories. They also investigate consumer complaints and furnish information about product safety. In addition, the agencies have the authority to order manufacturers to recall hazardous products.

Certification programs give consumers further information about product safety. For example, Underwriters Laboratories, Inc., a nonprofit organization, sets safety standards for building materials, electric appliances, and other products. It tests products submitted by manufacturers and awards a certifying seal to items that meet its standards.

Consumers can seek compensation in several ways for a loss or injury. For example, a person can sue by means of a *product liability suit* or a *malpractice suit.* A product liability suit is brought against a manufacturer or seller for damage or injury that is caused by a product. A malpractice suit is filed against an individual or a company in a service field, such as medicine or dentistry.

Consumers can file individual lawsuits in a regular court, or they can bring their claims to a *small-claims court.* Most small-claims courts handle consumer complaints involving up to $5,000. If many consumers have the same complaint, they may file their claims in a single lawsuit called a *class-action suit.*

People can also bring their complaints to consumer and business organizations. For example, many business companies finance organizations known as *better business bureaus.* The bureaus bring consumer complaints to the attention of business firms. Large numbers of companies have special departments that handle consumer problems. In addition, newspapers publish special columns, and radio and television stations broadcast programs that tell consumers how to make complaints.

The right to information. Advertising provides a major method by which manufacturers and sellers give information to consumers. The Federal Trade Commission (FTC) regulates advertising and administers several programs that handle deceptive claims. For example, the FTC may order a manufacturer to provide *corrective advertising* if misleading claims have been made.

The FTC and the state governments fight *bait-and-switch selling* and other deceptive sales methods. A bait-and-switch advertisement uses a special sale on a product as "bait" to attract customers to the advertiser's place of business. Salespeople then try to "switch" the customers to a more expensive product.

Name and Address	Description
Consumer Information Center (CIC) . . . . Pueblo, Colorado 81009	Offers over 200 free or low-cost pamphlets to consumers.
Consumer Product Safety Commission (CPSC). . . . . Washington, D.C. 20207	Sets safety standards for many household products.
Equal Employment Opportunity Commission (EEOC). . . . . . . Washington, D.C. 20506	Works to end job discrimination on the basis of race, color, sex, religion, age, and national origin.
Federal Communications Commission (FCC). . . . . 1919 M Street N.W. Washington, D.C. 20554	Regulates the radio and television industries.
Federal Trade Commission (FTC) . . . . Washington, D.C. 20580	Regulates advertising and administers programs that handle deceptive claims.
Food and Drug Administration (FDA). . . . . 5600 Fishers Lane Rockville, Maryland 20857	Enforces laws concerning the safety of food, drugs, and cosmetics.
Housing and Urban Development Department (HUD) . . . . 451 7th Street S.W. Washington, D.C. 20410	Investigates complaints concerning discrimination in buying or renting housing.
Occupational Safety and Health Administration (OSHA). . . . . Washington, D.C. 20210	Develops and enforces job safety and health standards for workers.

Various laws protect the consumer's right to adequate, truthful information. One of these laws is the Consumer Credit Protection Act of 1968, often called the Truth in Lending Act. It requires sellers to state clearly the charge made for loans and installment purchases and to express the interest rate as an annual rate. Another law affecting information given consumers is the Fair Packaging and Labeling Act of 1966, also known as the Truth in Packaging and Labeling Act. It requires that the package used for a product provide certain information. This information includes the identity of the product, the manufacturer's name and address, and the net quantity of the contents.

The United States Department of Agriculture requires that the grade of meat and dairy products appears on those items for the benefit of consumers. Many food stores use *unit pricing,* such as the price per ounce or per gram. This system helps consumers determine the best buy among several products in different sizes of packages. In addition, food manufacturers inform consumers by means of *freshness labeling,* also called *open dating.* A product is stamped with a date, which is the last day that it should be sold or used to assure quality or freshness.

Consumer organizations contribute much information about products. For example, Consumers' Research, Inc. and Consumers Union test a wide variety of products and publish the results. Consumers' Research is financed entirely by consumers who subscribe to its publications, and Consumers Union is supported chiefly by the sale of subscriptions, plus some contributions. Consumer groups also encourage the development of consumer education programs. Such programs emphasize the rights of consumers and provide information about managing money and making wise purchases.

The right to choose. The government regulates business in order to promote free and fair competition. The Sherman Antitrust Act of 1890 forbids monopolies.[3] The U.S. Department of Justice and the FTC enforce the Sherman Act. The FTC also enforces the Clayton Antitrust Act of 1914 and the Celler-Kefauver Act of 1950. These laws restrict businesses from forming combinations that might reduce competition. The Clayton Act also prohibits *price fixing,* a stated or implied agreement by several manufacturers to charge a noncompetitive price for a product they all make.

Some supporters of consumerism favor regulation by the FTC of the amount of money that businesses spend for advertising. They argue that small or new companies cannot spend large sums for advertising and thus cannot compete with large or older firms. As a result, businesses with larger advertising budgets have considerable control over the market and over the prices that consumers pay.

---

3. **monopolies:** companies or groups that have total control of a product or service, with power over prices and competition.

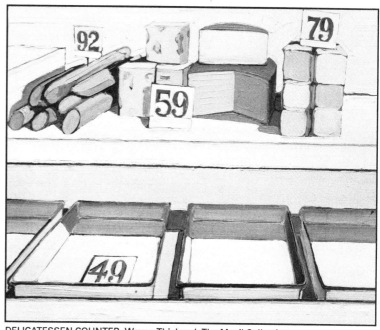

DELICATESSEN COUNTER, Wayne Thiebaud, The Menil Collection, Houston, Texas.

Have you ever bought more than you planned when grocery shopping? Read the following selection to learn more about ways supermarkets influence your buying decisions.

How to Save $2500 a Year in the Supermarket

When you push your shopping cart through the automatically opening door of a supermarket, you're walking into a selling machine. Every part of the supermarket—from the arrangement of the shelves to the placement of packages on the shelves to the packages themselves—is designed to sell. Much of what's being sold can't be eaten or used: For the mass-merchandising of food and other grocery products to succeed, you must be sold the value of inedible qualities such as a brand name's reputation.

By turning the supermarket into a selling machine, manufacturers and supermarket owners are hoping to influence in their favor the two-thirds of all buying decisions that aren't made until the shopper is actually in the store. It's hard work resisting all the pleas and sleeve-pluckings they build into the shopping experience. But the effort can cut the weekly tab by nearly half.

If you know how to defend yourself against the selling techniques used in the supermarket, you can save a lot. The first line of defense is to prepare a good, detailed shopping list and stick to it, no matter what. The next line of defense is to understand the supermarket in its role as selling machine.

The selling before you get there

Food companies and other manufacturers of products sold in the supermarket spend some $5 billion a year to soften you up before you ever enter the store. Most of that goes into TV commercials. One company alone—Procter & Gamble, maker of *Tide, Crest, Folgers, Crisco,* and many other familiar products—spends more than $1 billion a year on such persuasion. One reason manufacturers must pitch the products so hard: There are now too many brands, varieties, and sizes of products to fit on the shelves of even the largest supermarkets.

The crush of products makes it tough for shoppers to remember prices. Studies have shown that fewer than 10 percent of shoppers can estimate the correct price of any item in their cart. So manufacturers and supermarkets must increasingly remind shoppers when a price is a low price. Coupons are one way to do that—and the number of coupons surges yearly.

Coupons also help introduce new products, which manufacturers are turning out at a rate currently approaching 10,000 a year.

The selling inside the store

Using the store itself to help in the selling began when cracker companies took their crackers out of the cracker barrel and put them into boxes. Shoppers could pick up the box themselves, without needing a clerk to measure out their order. The "self-service grocery store" had been patented in 1917, but the idea of the supermarket didn't take off until the hard times of the Depression made people glad to give up service in return for a low price.

Michael Cullen, a grocery-store manager in Ohio, had a vision of a "cut-rate chain of wholesale stores selling direct to the public" that would sell some items at cost, others at 5 to 20 percent above cost. His idea was to make money by selling food at discount. If he made little or no profit on some items, he'd make a little more profit on others. Instead of clerks to remind customers of what to buy, the store itself would do it, with signs, displays, and shelves placed just so.

Cullen was able to try out the idea in his own store, a King Kullen in New York, in 1930. Supermarkets still work that way.

The package as advertisement

Product packages—the manufacturer's last chance to make its pitch—are often more important as advertisements than as containers. Laundry detergents like *Tide* take the direct approach and grab the eye with neon colors, huge letters, and shrieking claims.

But packaging can also add subtle values to a product. Colors such as black, burgundy, gold, or silver can be used to imply "elegance" or "style." A rough paper stock with type that looks like a wood-cut (as on *Classico* pasta sauce) can imply that the product is handmade.

A manufacturer can, by merely altering the package, "reposition" a product to appeal to a new sort of customer. The stainless-steel fork in the *Rice-A-Roni* package photo was recently replaced with a silver one to give the

Attractive packaging and eye-level positioning sell products.

package a more upscale look. *Breyers Ice Cream* got a new logo and a black carton for the same reason.

The money's in the mix

Anything a store does to make you notice a product is likely to increase its sales. Moving a brand from the bottom shelf to the prized eye-level position, for instance, has been shown to increase sales as much as 50 percent. It's no surprise, then, that the items at eye level tend to be items with a high profit margin—gourmet foods and other value-added items, as well as store brands. You'll find mayonnaise, flour, and pancake mix—staples you mean to buy, not impulse buys—on the lowest shelf.

A supermarket aims to make money on the mix of products, not on every single product—"merchandising the mix," it's called. The extra profit made

on a gourmet item might offset the small profit made on staples such as milk, coffee, sugar, potatoes, and detergent. Those high-demand items, in turn, can be advertised as "specials" or "leaders" to draw customers into the store, where they'll see champagne mustard and buy it instead of *French's*.

The mix can involve just a few products. Price the turkey low (if the price is too low to cover costs, it's a "loss leader"). Make up the money with the cranberries and stuffing mix in a tie-in display. Sell lettuce at cost, but make sure there's salad dressing on the shelf behind and a salad-serving set hanging from a hook above.

The mix involves entire departments. The service departments—produce, meat, dairy, and deli—generally make more money than dry foods and groceries, even though they cost more to

Merchandising the mix sells products.

run. They are typically located around the perimeter[1] of the store, partly because the location makes stocking easier, but also because the perimeter aisles are high-traffic aisles.

Perhaps you thought supermarkets were including video-tape rentals, cut flowers, or a pharmacy solely for your convenience? One-stop shopping is nice for the customer, but it also means the supermarket can include items whose markup is much higher than the overall supermarket average of about 20 percent. And supermarkets can still beat the prices of stores that deal in lower volume.

Store layout as the seller

It's not just the arrangement of products on the shelves that prompts you to buy. The supermarket must lead you to the shelves. As a food-marketing textbook puts it: "The rate of exposure is directly related to the rate of sale."

But a store can't be too manipulative—by forcing you to march along one long serpentine[2] aisle, say. As the textbook points out, "The overall objective . . . is to maximize sales and profit consistent with customer convenience." A store that makes itself too annoying will send its customers to other stores.

Early on, supermarkets began to use the gridiron[3] pattern of aisles as an efficient way to present the merchandise and use the space. There are several ways a supermarket can lead you past products it wants you to see:

• Start with a "power alley" just inside the door, filled with specials.

• Lead off with the produce department, since an attractive display showcases a store's image, and fruits

---

1. **perimeter:** outer boundary.
2. **serpentine:** winding, twisting.
3. **gridiron:** intersecting.

and vegetables are often bought on impulse.

• Locate the in-store bakery near the front of the store, so customers can smell it as soon as they step in.

• Put the milk at the back of the store so customers have to walk by plenty of products to get there. Put the frozen food cases on the way, since frozen foods are an impulse buy.

• Use end-aisle displays for products on sale. Or use them for products *not* on sale—customers often assume that anything so displayed is specially priced.

• Scatter sale items, high-profit merchandise, and popular products throughout the store. Put them half-way down the aisle so the shopper must walk by at least half the aisle's products to get there. Do the same with

End-aisle displays sell products.

free-standing displays or "shelf talkers," those little signs that point out a product on the shelf.

• Make aisles wide enough to feel expansive, but not so wide that shoppers can't easily be lured by both sides.

• Use island displays, open on all four sides, to slow traffic and let customers buy from all sides.

• Put a product in more than one place, so it must be resisted more than once.

• Display small impulse items with high margins—magazines, razors, candy, batteries—by the checkout counter.

The art of selling, refined

Part of the power of all those selling techniques derives from their utter familiarity—you walk by all the end-aisle displays and shelf-talkers every time you shop. Yet knowledge of how pitches are made can help give you the will to resist.

Supermarkets, however, are about to increase their knowledge of you the shopper considerably, through electronic price scanners. They may end up depriving you of one of your strongest weapons against selling—the ability to walk away.

Supermarkets switched to scanners to save on labor, the greatest expense in running a store. Chains are just beginning to reap scanners' informational benefits. No longer will supermarket managers have to estimate what sells best in their store. They'll know—and they'll know fast.

The computer running the cash register will also know what you

Displays by the checkout counter sell impulse items.

bought—knowledge that could allow supermarkets to target you, personally, with the kind of pitches you've been known to respond to. Scanners allow, for instance, coupons to be printed on the back of your receipt that vary according to what you buy. If information on what you buy should be linked up with your name and address—through, say, the debit card[4] or the electronically approved check-cashing card with which you pay for the groceries—marketers will be able to follow you home by mailing you customized pitches.

Such selling, while more insidious[5] than what presently occurs, demands the same defense: Keep your eyes open. Know what's going on. Shop smart. Buying the store brand can save you a lot

of money. Supermarkets don't provide you with store brands as a disinterested good deed. Store brands are a good deal for the supermarket, too. They often make more money for a store than higher-priced name-brand products.

The economics of the supermarket business explain that seeming paradox.[6] To attract customers, supermarkets often slash prices of well-known brands close to the supermarket's own cost. Competition among supermarkets helps keep the name-brand prices low.

Store brands are free of that kind of competition, and they often carry a higher profit margin. Not only do store brands build store profits, they build customer loyalty. You can buy *Mazola* just about anywhere. If you want *Grand Union* vegetable oil, you have to shop at a Grand Union. To encourage sales, supermarkets typically give store brands the prized eye-level position on the shelf.

Store brands can carry a lower price than name brands because the store saves on all the costs associated with promoting a brand, as well as on the quality of the product itself. Store brands essentially rely on the overall image and advertising of the store for their sales pitch. In turn, they can also be useful in selling a certain image for the store.

---

4. **debit card:** card by which money may be withdrawn or the cost of purchases paid directly from the holder's bank account.
5. **insidious:** clever and secretive.
6. **paradox:** contradiction.